I0781827

Pop Culture Trivia Large Print

Fun Facts and History Trivia Related to Pop Culture and the Celebrities Who Create It

Pop Culture Trivia

Trivia Questions and Answers Related to Pop Culture and the Celebrities Who Create It

Copyright 2024

Adicus Abbott

Your ultimate companion to the fascinating world of celebrity and pop culture trivia. This book is designed to take you on a thrilling journey through the highlights and hidden gems of movies, music, television, literature, and beyond. Whether you're a trivia buff, a pop culture enthusiast, or simply someone looking to impress friends with fun facts, this guide will provide both entertainment and enlightenment.

ISBN:9798333661074
Independently published

Table of Contents

Hollywood Pop Culture Trivia

Pop culture, particularly in Hollywood and the movie industry, is a dynamic tapestry woven with trends, icons, and narratives that captivate global audiences. It encompasses the cinematic zeitgeist, from blockbuster franchises that define generations to indie gems pushing creative boundaries.

Celebrities become cultural touchstones, their lives and scandals scrutinized as much as their on-screen performances. Red carpet events like the Oscars elevate films to artistry while shaping fashion trends worldwide. As digital platforms expand, streaming services democratize access, reshaping how we consume and discuss films.

Hollywood's influence extends beyond entertainment, shaping societal norms and reflecting our collective aspirations and anxieties. Test your knowledge of all things Hollywood with the following trivia questions and answers.

Q: Which 1994 film won the Academy Award for Best Picture and features the famous line "Life is like a box of chocolates"?
A: Forrest Gump

Q: Who directed the epic science fiction film "Inception"?
A: Christopher Nolan

Q: What is the highest-grossing film of all time, not adjusted for inflation?
A: Avatar

Q: Which movie features a computer named HAL 9000?
A: 2001: A Space Odyssey

Q: Who starred as the titular character in the 1981 film "Raiders of the Lost Ark"?
A: Harrison Ford

Q: Which 2019 film won the Palme d'Or at the Cannes Film Festival and the Academy Award for Best Picture?
A: Parasite

Q: What is the name of the kingdom where the 2013 Disney movie "Frozen" is set?
A: Arendelle

Q: Which director is known for films such as "Pulp Fiction" and "Kill Bill"?
A: Quentin Tarantino

Q: Who played the lead role in the 1990 film "Pretty Woman"?
A: Julia Roberts

Q: Which film features the iconic song "My Heart Will Go On" by Celine Dion?
A: Titanic

Q: What is the highest-grossing animated film of all time?
A: The Lion King (2019)

Q: Who directed the 1977 space opera "Star Wars"?
A: George Lucas

Q: Which film trilogy features characters named Frodo Baggins and Gandalf?
A: The Lord of the Rings

Q: Who won an Academy Award for Best Actress for her role in "La La Land"?
A: Emma Stone

Q: In which movie did Robert De Niro famously say, "You talkin' to me?"
A: Taxi Driver

Q: What film won the first Academy Award for Best Picture in 1929?
A: Wings

Q: Who directed the 1993 blockbuster "Jurassic Park"?
A: Steven Spielberg

Q: Which film features the quote, "Here's looking at you, kid"?
A: Casablanca

Q: Who starred as the Joker in the 2008 film "The Dark Knight"?
A: Heath Ledger

Q: Which movie is based on the life of mathematician John Nash?

A: A Beautiful Mind

Q: Who directed the 1994 animated film "The Lion King"?
A: Roger Allers and Rob Minkoff

Q: Which movie features a character named Jack Dawson?
A: Titanic

Q: What is the name of the hobbit played by Elijah Wood in "The Lord of the Rings" trilogy?
A: Frodo Baggins

Q: Who directed the 1999 horror film "The Sixth Sense"?
A: M. Night Shyamalan

Q: Which 2014 film features the song "Everything Is Awesome"?
A: The Lego Movie

Q: Who played the titular role in the 2001 film "Harry Potter and the Sorcerer's Stone"?
A: Daniel Radcliffe

Q: What 2008 film won eight Academy Awards, including Best Picture?
A: Slumdog Millionaire

Q: Who directed the 1980 horror film "The Shining"?
A: Stanley Kubrick

Q: In which film did Tom Hanks play a stranded man named Chuck Noland?
A: Cast Away

Q: What is the highest-grossing film directed by James Cameron?
A: Avatar

Q: Which movie features a dance competition in a 1950s-themed diner?
A: Pulp Fiction

Q: Who played the role of Katniss Everdeen in "The Hunger Games" series?
A: Jennifer Lawrence

Q: What 2015 film won the Academy Award for Best Picture and is set during the investigation of the Boston Globe into cases of widespread child abuse in the Catholic Church?
A: Spotlight

Q: Who directed the 1994 film "Pulp Fiction"?
A: Quentin Tarantino

Q: Which animated film features a rat named Remy who dreams of becoming a chef?
A: Ratatouille

Q: Who starred as the titular character in the 1999 film "The Matrix"?
A: Keanu Reeves

Q: Which movie features the iconic song "Over the Rainbow"?
A: The Wizard of Oz

Q: Who directed the 2017 horror film "Get Out"?
A: Jordan Peele

Q: In which film did Brad Pitt play a character named Tyler Durden?
A: Fight Club

Q: What is the highest-grossing film in the Marvel Cinematic Universe?
A: Avengers: Endgame

Q: Which movie features a group of friends who set out to find a missing boy named Will Byers?
A: Stranger Things (Note: This is a TV show, not a movie)

Q: Who directed the 2001 film "The Lord of the Rings: The Fellowship of the Ring"?
A: Peter Jackson

Q: Which film features the famous line "I'll be back"?
A: The Terminator

Q: Who starred as the titular character in the 2005 film "Batman Begins"?
A: Christian Bale

Q: What movie is about the life of Facebook founder Mark Zuckerberg?
A: The Social Network

Q: Who directed the 2018 film "Black Panther"?
A: Ryan Coogler

Q: In which film did Julia Roberts play a legal assistant named Erin Brockovich?
A: Erin Brockovich

Q: Which animated film features a cowboy doll named Woody and a space ranger named Buzz Lightyear?
A: Toy Story

Q: Who directed the 1994 film "Forrest Gump"?
A: Robert Zemeckis

Q: Which movie features a boxer named Rocky Balboa?
A: Rocky

Q: Who starred as Neo in "The Matrix" series?
A: Keanu Reeves

Q: What 2012 film is based on the true story of the hunt for Osama bin Laden?
A: Zero Dark Thirty

Q: Who directed the 2008 film "The Dark Knight"?
A: Christopher Nolan

Q: Which film features a lion named Simba and his journey to become king?
A: The Lion King

Q: Who starred as the titular character in the 1990 film "Edward Scissorhands"?
A: Johnny Depp

Q: Which movie features the song "Shallow," performed by Lady Gaga and Bradley Cooper?
A: A Star Is Born

Q: Who directed the 1999 film "American Beauty"?
A: Sam Mendes

Q: Which film franchise features the character Dom Toretto, played by Vin Diesel?
A: Fast & Furious

Q: Who directed the 2003 film "Lost in Translation"?
A: Sofia Coppola

Q: What is the highest-grossing film of 2022?
A: Top Gun: Maverick

Hollywood in the 1930s Pop Culture Trivia

The 1930s in Hollywood marked the Golden Age of cinema, introducing iconic stars like Clark Gable and Greta Garbo.

Landmark films such as "Gone with the Wind" and "The Wizard of Oz" defined the era, while innovative directors and the advent of sound revolutionized the movie industry. Put your thinking cap on and remember these golden years of Hollywood.

Q: Which 1939 film is known for the line "Frankly, my dear, I don't give a damn"?
A: "Gone with the Wind"

Q: Who starred as Scarlett O'Hara in "Gone with the Wind"?
A: Vivien Leigh

Q: What is the name of the 1933 film featuring a giant ape that climbs the Empire State Building?
A: "King Kong"

Q: Who played the title character in the 1931 film "Dracula"?
A: Bela Lugosi

Q: Which actress starred as Dorothy Gale in the 1939 classic "The Wizard of Oz"?
A: Judy Garland

Q: What 1934 Frank Capra film won the Academy Award for Best Picture?
A: "It Happened One Night"

Q: Who played the monster in the 1931 film "Frankenstein"?
A: Boris Karloff

Q: Which 1938 film was the first full-length animated feature by Walt Disney?
A: "Snow White and the Seven Dwarfs"

Q: Who starred as Rick Blaine in the 1931 film "Casablanca"?
A: Trick question: "Casablanca" was released in 1942. Humphrey Bogart starred as Rick Blaine.

Q: What is the title of the 1935 film where Clark Gable and Charles Laughton starred as Fletcher Christian and Captain Bligh?
A: "Mutiny on the Bounty"

Q: Who directed the 1939 film "Stagecoach," which helped make John Wayne a star?
A: John Ford

Q: In which 1939 film did Bette Davis play the character Julie Marsden?
A: "Jezebel"

Q: Who starred alongside Claudette Colbert in the 1934 film "It Happened One Night"?
A: Clark Gable

Q: Which 1936 Charlie Chaplin film is considered a satire on the machine age?
A: "Modern Times"

Q: What 1937 film features Fred Astaire and Ginger Rogers dancing to the song "Let's Face the Music and Dance"?
A: "Follow the Fleet"

Q: Who directed the 1932 horror film "Freaks"?
A: Tod Browning

Q: Which actress won the Academy Award for Best Actress for her role in the 1935 film "The Dark Angel"?
A: Katharine Hepburn

Q: What is the title of the 1931 film adaptation of Mary Shelley's novel about a scientist who creates life?
A: "Frankenstein"

Q: Who starred as the title character in the 1934 film "Cleopatra"?
A: Claudette Colbert

Q: Which 1939 film starred Henry Fonda as Tom Joad?
A: "The Grapes of Wrath"

Q: Who directed the 1935 film "Bride of Frankenstein"?
A: James Whale

Q: In which 1933 film did Katharine Hepburn make her film debut?
A: "A Bill of Divorcement"

Q: What is the name of the 1932 film starring Boris Karloff as an ancient Egyptian priest?
A: "The Mummy"

Q: Who starred opposite Ginger Rogers in the 1935 film "Top Hat"?
A: Fred Astaire

Q: Which 1939 film featured the song "Over the Rainbow"?
A: "The Wizard of Oz"

Q: Who played the role of Scarlett O'Hara's father in "Gone with the Wind"?
A: Thomas Mitchell

Q: What is the title of the 1937 film in which Marlene Dietrich played a saloon singer named Frenchy?
A: "Destry Rides Again"

Q: Who directed the 1930 film "All Quiet on the Western Front"?
A: Lewis Milestone

Q: Which 1938 film featured Errol Flynn as Robin Hood?
A: "The Adventures of Robin Hood"

Q: Who starred as the Tin Man in "The Wizard of Oz"?
A: Jack Haley

Q: What 1936 film features Paul Muni as the real-life French scientist Louis Pasteur?
A: "The Story of Louis Pasteur"

Q: Who played the title character in the 1933 film "The Invisible Man"?
A: Claude Rains

Q: Which 1932 film starred Fredric March as both Dr. Jekyll and Mr. Hyde?
A: "Dr. Jekyll and Mr. Hyde"

Q: What is the name of the 1939 film in which James Stewart plays a junior senator named Jefferson Smith?
A: "Mr. Smith Goes to Washington"

Q: Who directed the 1939 film "The Hunchback of Notre Dame"?
A: William Dieterle

Q: In which 1932 film did Greta Garbo famously say, "I want to be alone"?
A: "Grand Hotel"

Q: Which 1939 film starred Basil Rathbone as Sherlock Holmes?
A: "The Hound of the Baskervilles"

Q: Who played the role of the Scarecrow in "The Wizard of Oz"?
A: Ray Bolger

Q: What is the title of the 1934 film in which William Powell and Myrna Loy starred as Nick and Nora Charles?
A: "The Thin Man"

Q: Who directed the 1937 film "Snow White and the Seven Dwarfs"?
A: David Hand

Q: Which 1935 film featured Katharine Hepburn and Cary Grant in their first on-screen pairing?
A: "Sylvia Scarlett"

Q: Who played the title character in the 1931 film "Cimarron"?
A: Richard Dix

Q: What 1933 film starred Mae West and Cary Grant?
A: "She Done Him Wrong"

Q: Who starred as Frankenstein's Monster in the 1935 film "Bride of Frankenstein"?
A: Boris Karloff

Q: Which 1938 film starred Norma Shearer and Joan Crawford as rival friends?
A: "The Women"

Q: Who directed the 1934 film "The Scarlet Empress"?
A: Josef von Sternberg

Q: What is the title of the 1931 film in which Gary Cooper played a soldier during World War I?
A: "A Farewell to Arms"

Q: Who starred as the title character in the 1935 film "Captain Blood"?
A: Errol Flynn

Q: Which 1937 film featured Irene Dunne and Cary Grant as a couple going through a divorce?
A: "The Awful Truth"

Q: Who directed the 1939 film "Young Mr. Lincoln"?
A: John Ford

Q: What is the title of the 1932 film in which Lionel Barrymore plays an alcoholic attorney?
A: "A Free Soul"

Q: Who starred as the title character in the 1934 film "The Barretts of Wimpole Street"?
A: Norma Shearer

Q: Which 1939 film featured James Cagney as a dancer named George M. Cohan?
A: "Yankee Doodle Dandy"

Q: Who directed the 1937 film "Lost Horizon"?
A: Frank Capra

Q: What is the title of the 1935 film in which Fred Astaire and Ginger Rogers danced to "Cheek to Cheek"?
A: "Top Hat"

Q: Who starred as the title character in the 1932 film "The Most Dangerous Game"?
A: Joel McCrea

Q: Which

Q: Which 1939 film starred John Wayne as the Ringo Kid in his breakout role?
A: "Stagecoach"

Q: Who played the role of Rhett Butler in "Gone with the Wind"?
A: Clark Gable

Q: What is the title of the 1934 film in which William Powell played a detective named Philo Vance?
A: "The Thin Man"

Q: Who directed the 1931 film "M"?
A: Fritz Lang

Q: Which 1936 film starred Charlie Chaplin as a factory worker?
A: "Modern Times"

Q: Who starred as the title character in the 1935 film "David Copperfield"?
A: Freddie Bartholomew

Q: What is the title of the 1938 film that was the first major Technicolor release?
A: "The Adventures of Robin Hood"

Q: Who directed the 1939 film "The Wizard of Oz"?
A: Victor Fleming

Q: Which 1939 film featured Laurence Olivier as Heathcliff?
A: "Wuthering Heights"

Q: Who starred as the Invisible Man in the 1933 film "The Invisible Man"?
A: Claude Rains

Q: What is the title of the 1934 film in which Bette Davis played a scandalous actress?
A: "Of Human Bondage"

Q: Who directed the 1930 film "The Blue Angel"?
A: Josef von Sternberg

Q: Which 1932 film starred Jean Harlow and Clark Gable as lovers in a mining camp?
A: "Red Dust"

Q: Who played the role of Jane in the 1932 film "Tarzan the Ape Man"?
A: Maureen O'Sullivan

Q: Who starred as the title character in the 1932 film "Scarface"?
A: Paul Muni

Q: Which 1937 film starred Fred Astaire and Ginger Rogers as dancers in a New York hotel?
A: "Shall We Dance"

Q: Who directed the 1936 film "My Man Godfrey"?
A: Gregory La Cava

Q: What is the title of the 1933 film in which Katharine Hepburn played a pilot?
A: "Christopher Strong"

Q: Who starred as the title character in the 1934 film "The Merry Widow"?
A: Maurice Chevalier

Q: Which 1939 film featured a character named Rhett Butler?
A: "Gone with the Wind"

Q: Who directed the 1939 film "Mr. Smith Goes to Washington"?
A: Frank Capra

Q: What is the title of the 1938 film that starred Spencer Tracy and Mickey Rooney?
A: "Boys Town"

Q: Who starred as the title character in the 1931 film "Mata Hari"?
A: Greta Garbo

Q: Which 1932 film featured a love triangle between Greta Garbo, John Barrymore, and Joan Crawford?
A: "Grand Hotel"

Q: Who directed the 1934 film "It Happened One Night"?
A: Frank Capra

Q: What is the title of the 1935 film in which Fred Astaire and Ginger Rogers starred as a married couple on the brink of divorce?
A: "Top Hat"

Q: Which 1935 film starred Boris Karloff as the monster in "Bride of Frankenstein"?
A: "Bride of Frankenstein"

Hollywood in the 1940s Pop Culture Trivia

In the 1940s, Hollywood embraced film noir, war dramas, and musical extravaganzas, defining a decade shaped by World War II's impact. Stars like Humphrey Bogart and Ingrid Bergman became icons, while films such as "Casablanca" and "Citizen Kane" set new standards in storytelling and cinematography.

Hollywood's influence grew globally, shaping cultural narratives and reflecting societal changes amidst wartime and post-war optimism.

Q: Which 1942 film starring Humphrey Bogart and Ingrid Bergman is considered one of the greatest films of all time?
A: Casablanca

Q: What 1941 film, directed by and starring Orson Welles, is often cited as one of the best movies ever made?
A: Citizen Kane

Q: Who starred as Scarlett O'Hara in the 1939 film "Gone with the Wind," which continued to be popular in the 1940s?
A: Vivien Leigh

Q: Which 1946 Frank Capra film starring James Stewart has become a beloved Christmas classic?
A: It's a Wonderful Life

Q: What 1940 film marked the first time Charlie Chaplin spoke on screen?
A: The Great Dictator

Q: Which 1944 film noir featured Barbara Stanwyck and Fred MacMurray in a tale of insurance fraud and murder?
A: Double Indemnity

Q: What is the name of the 1941 animated Disney film about a flying elephant?
A: Dumbo

Q: Which actress starred opposite Humphrey Bogart in the 1944 film "To Have and Have Not"?
A: Lauren Bacall

Q: What 1949 film starring Olivia de Havilland earned her an Academy Award for Best Actress?
A: The Heiress

Q: Which Alfred Hitchcock film released in 1946 starred Cary Grant and Ingrid Bergman?
A: Notorious

Q: Who directed the 1942 horror film "Cat People"?
A: Jacques Tourneur

Q: Which 1945 film starring Joan Crawford won her an Academy Award for Best Actress?
A: Mildred Pierce

Q: What 1948 film stars John Wayne and Montgomery Clift as cowboys on a cattle drive?
A: Red River

Q: Which 1941 film stars Bette Davis as a repressed spinster who transforms her life after a romantic cruise?
A: Now, Voyager

Q: What 1940 romantic drama starred Laurence Olivier and Joan Fontaine and was directed by Alfred Hitchcock?
A: Rebecca

Q: Which 1946 film features a detective played by Humphrey Bogart and a femme fatale played by Lauren Bacall?
A: The Big Sleep

Q: What is the title of the 1944 film where Fred Astaire and Bing Crosby perform the song "White Christmas"?
A: Holiday Inn

Q: Which 1942 film features the iconic song "As Time Goes By"?
A: Casablanca

Q: Which 1940 film adaptation stars Henry Fonda as Tom Joad?
A: The Grapes of Wrath

Q: Who starred in the title role of the 1947 film "The Ghost and Mrs. Muir"?
A: Gene Tierney

Q: What 1948 movie stars Laurence Olivier in an adaptation of Shakespeare's tragedy?
A: Hamlet

Q: Which 1944 film features a psychological thriller directed by George Cukor starring Ingrid Bergman?
A: Gaslight

Q: What 1945 romantic drama stars Gregory Peck and Ingrid Bergman and is set in a psychiatric hospital?
A: Spellbound

Q: Which 1946 film noir stars Robert Mitchum and Jane Greer in a tale of love and betrayal?
A: Out of the Past

Q: What 1941 movie stars James Cagney as a gangster and features the famous line "Made it, Ma! Top of the world!"?
A: White Heat

Q: Who starred opposite Judy Garland in the 1944 musical "Meet Me in St. Louis"?
A: Margaret O'Brien

Q: What 1942 film stars Katharine Hepburn as a political activist opposite Spencer Tracy as a sportswriter?
A: Woman of the Year

Q: Which 1948 film features Ingrid Bergman as a pianist and Charles Boyer as her sinister husband?
A: Gaslight

Q: What 1949 film directed by Carol Reed stars Orson Welles and Joseph Cotten in post-war Vienna?

A: The Third Man

Q: Who played the title role in the 1944 film "Laura"?
A: Gene Tierney

Q: What 1941 film stars Barbara Stanwyck as a con
artist and Henry Fonda as her gullible victim?
A: The Lady Eve

Q: Which 1943 film stars Humphrey Bogart as a ship
captain involved in a love triangle during World War II?
A: Action in the North Atlantic

Q: What 1944 film features Judy Garland performing
the song "Have Yourself a Merry Little Christmas"?
A: Meet Me in St. Louis

Q: Which 1949 movie directed by John Ford stars
John Wayne and features the story of the U.S. Cavalry?
A: She Wore a Yellow Ribbon

Q: Who starred opposite Gregory Peck in the 1949
war film "Twelve O'Clock High"?
A: Dean Jagger

Q: What 1945 film stars Joan Crawford in a role that
earned her an Academy Award for Best Actress?
A: Mildred Pierce

Q: Which 1942 film features Cary Grant as a
newspaper editor and Rosalind Russell as his ex-wife?
A: His Girl Friday

Q: What 1940 film stars Bette Davis as a Southern
belle who defies her family to marry the man she loves?
A: The Letter

Q: Who played the title character in the 1942 biographical film "Yankee Doodle Dandy"?
A: James Cagney

Q: Which 1947 film features Rita Hayworth performing the song "Put the Blame on Mame"?
A: Gilda

Q: What 1944 film stars Ingrid Bergman and Charles Boyer in a suspenseful drama about gaslighting?
A: Gaslight

Q: Which 1948 film stars Humphrey Bogart as a down-and-out gold prospector in Mexico?
A: The Treasure of the Sierra Madre

Q: Who directed the 1945 film "The Bells of St. Mary's" starring Bing Crosby and Ingrid Bergman?
A: Leo McCarey

Q: What 1941 movie stars Katharine Hepburn as a free-spirited woman who falls in love with a strait-laced man?
A: The Philadelphia Story

Q: Which 1946 film noir stars Alan Ladd and Veronica Lake in a tale of murder and deception?
A: The Blue Dahlia

Q: What 1943 film stars Humphrey Bogart and Claude Rains in a wartime romance?
A: Casablanca

Q: Who starred opposite Judy Garland in the 1944 musical "Meet Me in St. Louis"?

A: Tom Drake

Q: What 1945 film stars Gene Tierney as a murderously jealous wife?
A: Leave Her to Heaven

Q: What 1948 film stars Spencer Tracy as a father dealing with his daughter's wedding preparations?
A: Father of the Bride

Q: Which 1940 film features Laurence Olivier as Heathcliff and Merle Oberon as Cathy?
A: Wuthering Heights

Q: What 1942 film stars Greer Garson and Walter Pidgeon as a British couple during World War II?
A: Mrs. Miniver

Q: Which 1944 film stars Barbara Stanwyck as a manipulative femme fatale?
A: Double Indemnity

Q: What 1940 film features a musical score by Aaron Copland and stars Henry Fonda?
A: The Grapes of Wrath

Q: Who played the title role in the 1948 film "Joan of Arc"?
A: Ingrid Bergman

Q: Which 1947 film stars Robert Mitchum and Jane Greer in a film noir classic?
A: Out of the Past

Q: What 1946 film features a post-war mystery involving a group of friends in Washington, D.C.?

A: The Best Years of Our Lives

Q: Which 1940 film stars Bette Davis as a governess who falls in love with her employer?
A: The Letter

Q: What 1949 film stars James Stewart as a father who becomes involved in a cattle drive?
A: Winchester '73

Q: Which 1944 film stars Fred MacMurray as an insurance salesman involved in a murder plot?
A: Double Indemnity

Q: What 1941 movie stars Cary Grant as a newspaper editor trying to win back his ex-wife?
A: His Girl Friday

Q: Who directed the 1945 film "The Lost Weekend," which won the Academy Award for Best Picture?
A: Billy Wilder

Q: Which 1942 film stars Ginger Rogers as a woman who disguises herself as a teenager?
A: The Major and the Minor

Q: What 1947 film stars Gregory Peck as a reporter posing as a Jew to expose anti-Semitism?
A: Gentleman's Agreement

Q: Who starred as George Bailey in the 1946 film "It's a Wonderful Life"?
A: James Stewart

Q: Which 1941 film stars Joan Fontaine as a young bride haunted by her husband's first wife?

A: Rebecca

Q: What 1944 film stars Bing Crosby as a priest trying
to save a run-down church?
A: Going My Way

Q: Which 1949 film stars Ingrid Bergman as a nun
struggling with her faith?
A: The Bells of St. Mary's

Q: What 1946 film features a post-war romance
between an American soldier and a British woman?
A: The Best Years of Our Lives

Q: Which 1942 film stars Katharine Hepburn and
Spencer Tracy in a battle of the sexes?
A: Woman of the Year

Q: What 1945 film stars Ingrid Bergman as a
psychiatrist who falls in love with a patient?
A: Spellbound

Q: Which 1941 film stars Fred Astaire and Rita
Hayworth in a musical romance?
A: You'll Never Get Rich

Q: What 1948 film stars Laurence Olivier as a prince
who must avenge his father's death?
A: Hamlet

Q: Which 1944 film stars Barbara Stanwyck as a
manipulative femme fatale in a film noir classic?
A: Double Indemnity

Q: What 1941 film stars Bette Davis as a Southern
belle who defies her family to marry the man she loves?

A: The Little Foxes

Q: Who played the title role in the 1947 film "The Ghost and Mrs. Muir"?
A: Gene Tierney

Q: Which 1949 film stars James Stewart as a struggling lawyer defending an innocent man?
A: The Stratton Story

Q: What 1943 film stars Humphrey Bogart as a ship captain involved in a wartime love triangle?
A: Action in the North Atlantic

Q: Which 1945 film stars Joan Crawford in a role that earned her an Academy Award for Best Actress?
A: Mildred Pierce

Q: What 1942 film features Cary Grant as a newspaper editor and Rosalind Russell as his ex wife?
A: His Girl Friday

Q: Which 1944 film stars Ingrid Bergman and Charles Boyer in a suspenseful drama about gaslighting?
A: Gaslight

Q: What 1948 film stars Humphrey Bogart as a down-and-out gold prospector in Mexico?
A: The Treasure of the Sierra Madre

Q: Who directed the 1945 film "The Bells of St. Mary's" starring Bing Crosby and Ingrid Bergman?
A: Leo McCarey

Q: Which 1941 film stars Katharine Hepburn as a free-spirited woman who falls in love with a strait-laced man?
A: The Philadelphia Story

Q: What 1946 film noir stars Alan Ladd and Veronica Lake in a tale of murder and deception?
A: The Blue Dahlia

Q: Which 1943 film stars Humphrey Bogart and Claude Rains in a wartime romance?
A: Casablanca

Q: Who starred opposite Judy Garland in the 1944 musical "Meet Me in St. Louis"?
A: Tom Drake

Q: What 1945 film stars Gene Tierney as a murderously jealous wife?
A: Leave Her to Heaven

Q: Which 1942 film features Gary Cooper as a decorated World War I hero?
A: Sergeant York

Q: What 1948 film stars Spencer Tracy as a father dealing with his daughter's wedding preparations?
A: Father of the Bride

Q: Which 1940 film features Laurence Olivier as Heathcliff and Merle Oberon as Cathy?
A: Wuthering Heights

Q: What 1942 film stars Greer Garson and Walter Pidgeon as a British couple during World War II?
A: Mrs. Miniver

Q: Which 1944 film stars Barbara Stanwyck as a manipulative femme fatale?
A: Double Indemnity

Q: What 1940 film features a musical score by Aaron Copland and stars Henry Fonda?
A: The Grapes of Wrath

Q: Who played the title role in the 1948 film "Joan of Arc"?
A: Ingrid Bergman

Q: Which 1947 film stars Robert Mitchum and Jane Greer in a film noir classic?
A: Out of the Past

Q: What 1946 film features a post-war mystery involving a group of friends in Washington, D.C.?
A: The Best Years of Our Lives

Hollywood in the 1950s Pop Culture Trivia

In the 1950s, Hollywood experienced a diverse cinematic landscape, from the rise of rebellious youth culture in films like "Rebel Without a Cause" to the golden era of musicals with stars like Marilyn Monroe and James Dean.

Cold War anxieties influenced sci-fi and horror genres, while method acting and new film making techniques emerged. Hollywood's reach expanded globally, cementing its role as a cultural powerhouse and reflecting America's evolving social dynamics.

Q: Which 1952 musical features Gene Kelly dancing in the rain?
A: Singin' in the Rain

Q: Who starred as the rebellious teenager Jim Stark in the 1955 film "Rebel Without a Cause"?
A: James Dean

Q: What 1954 film stars Marlon Brando as a longshoreman who "could have been a contender"?
A: On the Waterfront

Q: Which 1950 film stars Bette Davis as an aging Broadway star named Margo Channing?
A: All About Eve

Q: What 1953 film features Marilyn Monroe singing "Diamonds Are a Girl's Best Friend"?
A: Gentlemen Prefer Blondes

Q: Who directed the 1959 epic film "Ben-Hur"?
A: William Wyler

Q: Which 1958 Hitchcock film stars James Stewart and Kim Novak in a psychological thriller set in San Francisco?
A: Vertigo

Q: What 1951 film stars Vivien Leigh and Marlon Brando and is based on a play by Tennessee Williams?
A: A Streetcar Named Desire

Q: Who starred opposite Audrey Hepburn in the 1953 romantic comedy "Roman Holiday"?
A: Gregory Peck

Q: Which 1956 science fiction film features a crew encountering a mysterious alien civilization on the planet Altair IV?
A: Forbidden Planet

Q: What 1955 musical stars Gordon MacRae and Shirley Jones and is set in the Oklahoma Territory?
A: Oklahoma!

Q: Who directed the 1954 film "Rear Window" starring James Stewart and Grace Kelly?
A: Alfred Hitchcock

Q: Which 1956 epic film stars Charlton Heston as Moses?

A: The Ten Commandments

Q: What 1957 film features Henry Fonda as a lone juror standing up for justice?
A: 12 Angry Men

Q: Who starred as the titular character in the 1954 film "Carmen Jones"?
A: Dorothy Dandridge

Q: Which 1955 film features the song "Rock Around the Clock" by Bill Haley & His Comets?
A: Blackboard Jungle

Q: What 1959 comedy stars Marilyn Monroe, Tony Curtis, and Jack Lemmon in a story about musicians in drag?
A: Some Like It Hot

Q: Who directed the 1953 western "Shane" starring Alan Ladd?
A: George Stevens

Q: Which 1951 science fiction film features an alien named Klaatu and his robot Gort?
A: The Day the Earth Stood Still

Q: What 1958 film stars Paul Newman as a troubled Southern youth named Brick Pollitt?
A: Cat on a Hot Tin Roof

Q: Who starred as Norma Desmond in the 1950 film "Sunset Boulevard"?
A: Gloria Swanson

Q: Which 1956 film stars Deborah Kerr and Yul Brynner and is set in the court of Siam?
A: The King and I

Q: What 1959 film stars Cary Grant as an advertising executive mistaken for a spy?
A: North by Northwest

Q: Who directed the 1957 film "The Bridge on the River Kwai"?
A: David Lean

Q: Which 1953 film features Marlon Brando as a rebellious motorcycle gang leader?
A: The Wild One

Q: What 1958 musical stars Rosalind Russell as a free-spirited woman who takes in her nephew?
A: Auntie Mame

Q: Who starred as Billy the Kid in the 1958 film "The Left Handed Gun"?
A: Paul Newman

Q: Which 1951 film features Humphrey Bogart and Katharine Hepburn on a steamboat adventure in Africa?
A: The African Queen

Q: What 1959 film stars Audrey Hepburn as a nun struggling with her faith?
A: The Nun's Story

Q: Who directed the 1954 monster movie "Godzilla"?
A: Ishirō Honda

Q: Which 1950 film stars Judy Holliday as a ditsy blonde who learns to outwit her boyfriend?
A: Born Yesterday

Q: What 1957 film stars Elvis Presley as a singing race car driver?
A: Jailhouse Rock

Q: Who starred opposite James Dean in the 1955 film "East of Eden"?
A: Julie Harris

Q: Which 1956 film stars Deborah Kerr and Burt Lancaster in a passionate beach scene?
A: From Here to Eternity

Q: What 1958 film stars Ingrid Bergman as a troubled nun?
A: The Inn of the Sixth Happiness

Q: Who directed the 1957 musical "West Side Story"?
A: Jerome Robbins and Robert Wise

Q: Which 1959 film features a chariot race and stars Charlton Heston?
A: Ben-Hur

Q: What 1950 film stars James Stewart as a man whose best friend is an invisible rabbit?
A: Harvey

Q: Who starred as Maggie the Cat in the 1958 film "Cat on a Hot Tin Roof"?
A: Elizabeth Taylor

Q: Which 1954 Hitchcock film stars Grace Kelly and Ray Milland in a plot to commit the perfect murder?
A: Dial M for Murder

Q: What 1957 film stars Henry Fonda and Charles Bronson in a tale of vigilante justice?
A: 12 Angry Men

Q: Who directed the 1954 film "On the Waterfront"?
A: Elia Kazan

Q: Which 1953 film stars Gregory Peck as a captain on a naval destroyer during World War II?
A: The Caine Mutiny

Q: What 1955 film features Frank Sinatra as a drug addict trying to go straight?
A: The Man with the Golden Arm

Q: Who starred opposite Audrey Hepburn in the 1954 film "Sabrina"?
A: Humphrey Bogart

Q: Which 1958 film stars Cary Grant and Ingrid Bergman in a romantic thriller about spies?
A: Indiscreet

Q: What 1957 film stars Deborah Kerr and Cary Grant in a romance that culminates at the Empire State Building?
A: An Affair to Remember

Q: Who starred as the titular character in the 1951 film "The African Queen"?
A: Humphrey Bogart

Q: Which 1953 film features Marilyn Monroe, Jane Russell, and a song about diamonds?
A: Gentlemen Prefer Blondes

Q: What 1959 film stars Simone Signoret and Véra Clouzot in a tale of murder at a boarding school?
A: Les Diaboliques

Q: Who starred as the lead character in the 1952 film "High Noon"?
A: Gary Cooper

Q: Which 1954 film features Marlon Brando as an ex-boxer turned longshoreman?
A: On the Waterfront

Q: What 1958 musical features Leslie Caron as a young girl groomed to be a courtesan?
A: Gigi

Q: Who directed the 1950 film "Sunset Boulevard"?
A: Billy Wilder

Q: Which 1957 film stars Alec Guinness as a British colonel in a Japanese POW camp?
A: The Bridge on the River Kwai

Q: What 1953 film stars John Wayne and Geraldine Page in a western set in Texas?
A: Hondo

Q: Who starred opposite Grace Kelly in the 1955 film "To Catch a Thief"?
A: Cary Grant

Q: Which 1951 film stars Marlon Brando and Vivien Leigh in a steamy New Orleans drama?
A: A Streetcar Named Desire

Q: What 1956 film stars Ingrid Bergman and Yul Brynner as lovers from different cultures?
A: Anastasia

Q: Who directed the 1959 comedy "Some Like It Hot"?
A: Billy Wilder

Q: Which 1953 film stars Elizabeth Taylor as a young woman caught in a love triangle?
A: The Girl Who Had Everything

Hollywood in the 1960s Pop Culture Trivia

The 1960s in Hollywood marked a transformative era of cinematic experimentation and cultural upheaval. Icons like Audrey Hepburn and Paul Newman defined the decade with films ranging from groundbreaking classics like "Psycho" and "The Graduate" to epic spectacles like "Lawrence of Arabia."

Filmmakers embraced new themes of rebellion, social change, and the counterculture, reflecting the era's political turmoil and pushing artistic boundaries in storytelling and film making techniques.

Q: Which 1961 film stars Audrey Hepburn as Holly Golightly?
A: Breakfast at Tiffany's

Q: Who directed the 1960 thriller "Psycho"?
A: Alfred Hitchcock

Q: What 1965 musical features Julie Andrews as a singing nun turned governess?
A: The Sound of Music

Q: Which 1967 film stars Sidney Poitier as a detective in Mississippi?
A: In the Heat of the Night

Q: Who starred opposite Paul Newman in the 1967 film "Cool Hand Luke"?
A: George Kennedy

Q: What 1968 film features Charlton Heston discovering a post-apocalyptic world ruled by apes?
A: Planet of the Apes

Q: Which 1963 film stars Elizabeth Taylor and Richard Burton as the Queen of Egypt and her Roman lover?
A: Cleopatra

Q: Who directed the 1964 film "Dr. Strangelove"?
A: Stanley Kubrick

Q: What 1969 film stars Dustin Hoffman and Jon Voight as hustlers in New York City?
A: Midnight Cowboy

Q: Which 1962 film stars Gregory Peck as the lawyer Atticus Finch?
A: To Kill a Mockingbird

Q: Who starred as James Bond in the 1962 film "Dr. No"?
A: Sean Connery

Q: What 1967 film features Faye Dunaway and Warren Beatty as notorious bank robbers?
A: Bonnie and Clyde

Q: Which 1968 musical stars Barbra Streisand as a rising singer in the Ziegfeld Follies?
A: Funny Girl

Q: Who directed the 1960 epic film "Spartacus"?

A: Stanley Kubrick

Q: What 1965 film stars Omar Sharif as a Russian physician and poet?
A: Doctor Zhivago

Q: Which 1968 film features a computer named HAL 9000?
A: 2001: A Space Odyssey

Q: Who starred as Maria in the 1961 film "West Side Story"?
A: Natalie Wood

Q: What 1966 film stars Steve McQueen as a wealthy thief?
A: The Thomas Crown Affair

Q: Which 1963 film features Peter Sellers in multiple roles, including President Merkin Muffley?
A: Dr. Strangelove

Q: Who directed the 1969 film "Butch Cassidy and the Sundance Kid"?
A: George Roy Hill

Q: What 1964 film stars Audrey Hepburn and Rex Harrison in a story about a flower girl and a phonetics professor?
A: My Fair Lady

Q: Which 1967 film features Anne Bancroft as a seductive older woman?
A: The Graduate

Q: Who starred opposite Paul Newman in the 1961 film "The Hustler"?
A: Jackie Gleason

Q: What 1963 film stars Steve McQueen in a daring motorcycle escape from a POW camp?
A: The Great Escape

Q: Which 1966 film stars Elizabeth Taylor and Richard Burton as a combative married couple?
A: Who's Afraid of Virginia Woolf?

Q: Who directed the 1969 Western "The Wild Bunch"?
A: Sam Peckinpah

Q: What 1962 film stars Bette Davis and Joan Crawford as two feuding sisters?
A: What Ever Happened to Baby Jane?

Q: Which 1965 film stars Julie Christie as a woman navigating complex romantic relationships in 1960s London?
A: Darling

Q: Who starred as the titular character in the 1963 film "Cleopatra"?
A: Elizabeth Taylor

Q: What 1969 film stars Peter Fonda and Dennis Hopper as two bikers traveling across America?
A: Easy Rider

Q: Which 1968 film stars Jack Lemmon and Walter Matthau in a comedic adaptation of a Neil Simon play?
A: The Odd Couple

Q: Who directed the 1961 film "Judgment at Nuremberg"?
A: Stanley Kramer

Q: What 1964 film stars Sean Connery as James Bond, facing off against a villain with a deadly hat?
A: Goldfinger

Q: Which 1966 film features Clint Eastwood as a mysterious drifter known as "The Man with No Name"?
A: The Good, the Bad and the Ugly

Q: Who starred opposite Audrey Hepburn in the 1964 romantic comedy "Paris When It Sizzles"?
A: William Holden

Q: What 1963 film features Alfred Hitchcock's chilling tale of bird attacks in a small town?
A: The Birds

Q: Which 1967 film stars Sidney Poitier as a teacher in a tough London school?
A: To Sir, with Love

Q: Who directed the 1969 musical "Hello, Dolly!" starring Barbra Streisand?
A: Gene Kelly

Q: What 1965 film stars Rex Harrison as a linguistics professor and Audrey Hepburn as his pupil?
A: My Fair Lady

Q: Which 1960 film stars Jack Lemmon and Shirley MacLaine in a romantic comedy about an office worker and an elevator operator?

A: The Apartment

Q: Who starred as the titular character in the 1968 film "Rosemary's Baby"?
A: Mia Farrow

Q: What 1967 film stars Paul Newman and Robert Redford as two outlaws on the run?
A: Butch Cassidy and the Sundance Kid

Q: Which 1962 film features Gregory Peck as a lawyer defending a black man accused of raping a white woman in the Deep South?
A: To Kill a Mockingbird

Q: Who starred as the titular character in the 1965 film "The Agony and the Ecstasy"?
A: Charlton Heston

Q: What 1968 film stars Peter Sellers as a bumbling French detective?
A: The Pink Panther

Q: Which 1961 film stars Natalie Wood and Richard Beymer in a musical adaptation of "Romeo and Juliet"?
A: West Side Story

Q: Who directed the 1964 film "Mary Poppins"?
A: Robert Stevenson

Q: What 1967 film stars Warren Beatty and Faye Dunaway as notorious bank robbers?
A: Bonnie and Clyde

Q: Which 1966 film stars Paul Scofield as Sir Thomas More?

A: A Man for All Seasons

Q: Who starred opposite Julie Andrews in the 1964 film "The Americanization of Emily"?
A: James Garner

Q: What 1968 film stars Jane Fonda as a space-traveling heroine?
A: Barbarella

Q: Which 1960 film features Audrey Hepburn as a blind woman terrorized by criminals?
A: Wait Until Dark

Q: Who directed the 1966 film "Fahrenheit 451"?
A: François Truffaut

Q: What 1963 film stars Cary Grant and Audrey Hepburn in a romantic thriller set in Paris?
A: Charade

Q: Which 1969 film features Robert Redford and Paul Newman as two con men?
A: Butch Cassidy and the Sundance Kid

Q: Who starred as the titular character in the 1961 film "Breakfast at Tiffany's"?
A: Audrey Hepburn

Q: What 1967 film stars Katharine Hepburn and Spencer Tracy in a story about interracial marriage?
A: Guess Who's Coming to Dinner

Q: Which 1966 film stars Michael Caine as a promiscuous Londoner?
A: Alfie

Q: Who directed the 1964 film "A Hard Day's Night" starring The Beatles?
A: Richard Lester

Q: What 1965 film stars Julie Christie and Omar Sharif in a love story set against the Russian Revolution?
A: Doctor Zhivago

Q: Which 1961 film stars Frank Sinatra and Dean Martin as part of a gang planning a Las Vegas heist?
A: Ocean's 11

Q: Who starred opposite Audrey Hepburn in the 1967 film "Two for the Road"?
A: Albert Finney

Q: What 1962 film features Peter O'Toole as a British officer during World War I?
A: Lawrence of Arabia

Q: Which 1963 film stars Jerry Lewis as a klutzy professor who transforms into a suave swinger?
A: The Nutty Professor

Q: Who directed the 1960 film "The Magnificent Seven"?
A: John Sturges

Q: What 1967 film stars Dustin Hoffman as a college graduate seduced by an older woman?
A: The Graduate

Q: Which 1965 film stars Sean Connery as James Bond thwarting an evil organization's plan to rob Fort Knox?
A: Goldfinger

Q: Who starred as Maria in the 1965 film "The Sound of Music"?
A: Julie Andrews

Q: What 1969 film stars Michael Caine as a British spy investigating a murder in Berlin?
A: Funeral in Berlin

Q: Which 1964 film stars Peter Sellers as a bumbling French detective?
A: A Shot in the Dark

Q: Who directed the 1967 film "In the Heat of the Night"?
A: Norman Jewison

Q: What 1962 film stars Gregory Peck as Atticus Finch in a courtroom drama?
A: To Kill a Mockingbird

Q: Which 1963 film stars Cary Grant and Doris Day in a romantic comedy about a misunderstood affair?
A: That Touch of Mink

Q: Who starred opposite Steve McQueen in the 1968 film "Bullitt"?
A: Jacqueline Bisset

Q: What 1961 film features Audrey Hepburn as a New York socialite and George Peppard as a struggling writer?
A: Breakfast at Tiffany's

Q: Which 1964 film stars Julie Andrews as a magical nanny?

A: Mary Poppins

Q: Who directed the 1968 film "2001: A Space Odyssey"?
A: Stanley Kubrick

Q: What 1965 film stars Omar Sharif as a Russian poet and doctor during the Russian Revolution?
A: Doctor Zhivago

Q: Which 1963 film features a famous motorcycle chase scene starring Steve McQueen?
A: The Great Escape

Q: Who starred as James Bond in the 1964 film "Goldfinger"?
A: Sean Connery

Q: What 1967 film stars Anne Bancroft as a seductive older woman and Dustin Hoffman as a recent college graduate?
A: The Graduate

Q: Which 1969 film stars Robert Redford and Paul Newman as two charming outlaws?
A: Butch Cassidy and the Sundance Kid

Q: Who directed the 1964 film "My Fair Lady"?
A: George Cukor

Q: What 1968 film stars Mia Farrow as a woman who believes her unborn child is in danger from a cult?
A: Rosemary's Baby

Q: Which 1960 film stars Jack Lemmon and Shirley MacLaine in a story about an office worker and an elevator operator?
A: The Apartment

Q: Who starred as the titular character in the 1964 film "Mary Poppins"?
A: Julie Andrews

Q: What 1966 film stars Clint Eastwood as a mysterious drifter known as "The Man with No Name"?
A: The Good, the Bad and the Ugly

Q: Which 1961 film features a rivalry between two New York City gangs?
A: West Side Story

Q: Who directed the 1960 film "Psycho"?
A: Alfred Hitchcock

Q: What 1963 film stars Elizabeth Taylor and Richard Burton as the Queen of Egypt and her Roman lover?
A: Cleopatra

Q: Which 1967 film stars Sidney Poitier as a detective in Mississippi?
A: In the Heat of the Night

Q: Who starred opposite Paul Newman in the 1967 film "Cool Hand Luke"?
A: George Kennedy

Q: Which 1962 film stars Gregory Peck as a lawyer defending a black man accused of raping a white woman in the Deep South?

A: To Kill a Mockingbird

Q: Who starred opposite Audrey Hepburn in the 1964 romantic comedy "Paris When It Sizzles"?
A: William Holden

Q: What 1964 film stars Sean Connery as James Bond, facing off against a villain with a deadly hat?
A: Goldfinger

Q: Which 1966 film stars Elizabeth Taylor and Richard Burton as a combative married couple?
A: Who's Afraid of Virginia Woolf?

Q: Who directed the 1965 musical "The Sound of Music"?
A: Robert Wise

Q: What 1967 film stars Warren Beatty and Faye Dunaway as notorious bank robbers?
A: Bonnie and Clyde

Q: Which 1968 film stars Steve McQueen as a detective investigating a murder in San Francisco?
A: Bullitt

Television Pop Culture Trivia

Pop culture in television thrives on a diverse landscape of genres and iconic shows that resonate deeply with audiences worldwide. From binge-worthy dramas like "Game of Thrones" to groundbreaking comedies like "Friends," TV shapes cultural conversations and defines eras. Reality TV transforms everyday people into celebrities, while competition shows captivate with skill and drama. Streaming services revolutionize viewing habits, offering original content that challenges traditional formats. Social media amplifies fan support, fostering communities around favorite characters and storylines. In short, television shows and the actors who lay on them are a part of our lives.

TV not only entertains but also reflects societal shifts, sparking dialogue on politics, identity, and global issues. In an era of peak TV, television remains a powerful mirror reflecting our shared experiences and evolving cultural landscape.

Q: What is the name of the coffee shop where the friends frequently hang out in "Friends"?
A: Central Perk

Q: Which TV show features a high school chemistry teacher turned methamphetamine manufacturer?
A: Breaking Bad

Q: Who played the character of Sheldon Cooper in "The Big Bang Theory"?
A: Jim Parsons

Q: In "The Office," what is the name of the paper company where the characters work?
A: Dunder Mifflin

Q: Which show revolves around the political career of Frank Underwood?
A: House of Cards

Q: What is the name of the fictional town where "Stranger Things" is set?
A: Hawkins

Q: Who is the creator of "The Simpsons"?
A: Matt Groening

Q: What is the name of the bar where the characters of "How I Met Your Mother" frequently meet?
A: MacLaren's Pub

Q: Which TV series features a character named Don Draper?
A: Mad Men

Q: Who played the character of Walter White in "Breaking Bad"?
A: Bryan Cranston

Q: What is the name of the fictional town in "Parks and Recreation"?
A: Pawnee

Q: Which TV show features a character named Liz Lemon?
A: 30 Rock

Q: Who played the role of Rachel Green in "Friends"?
A: Jennifer Aniston

Q: What is the name of the spaceship in "Firefly"?
A: Serenity

Q: Which TV series is known for the quote "Winter is coming"?
A: Game of Thrones

Q: Who played the character of Buffy Summers in "Buffy the Vampire Slayer"?
A: Sarah Michelle Gellar

Q: What is the name of the diner in "Seinfeld"?
A: Monk's Café

Q: Which TV show features a character named Eleven with telekinetic powers?
A: Stranger Things

Q: Who played the role of Tyrion Lannister in "Game of Thrones"?
A: Peter Dinklage

Q: What is the name of the family dog in "Family Guy"?
A: Brian

Q: Which TV show features a character named Michael Scott?
A: The Office

Q: Who played the character of Olivia Pope in "Scandal"?
A: Kerry Washington

Q: What is the name of the fictional high school in "Glee"?
A: William McKinley High School

Q: Which TV series features a group of survivors in a post-apocalyptic world overrun by zombies?
A: The Walking Dead

Q: Who played the character of Daenerys Targaryen in "Game of Thrones"?
A: Emilia Clarke

Q: What is the name of the animated series featuring a dysfunctional family living in Springfield?
A: The Simpsons

Q: Which TV show is set in the fictional town of Stars Hollow?
A: Gilmore Girls

Q: Who played the character of Tony Soprano in "The Sopranos"?
A: James Gandolfini

Q: What is the name of the fictional advertising agency in "Mad Men"?
A: Sterling Cooper

Q: Which TV series features a time-traveling alien called the Doctor?
A: Doctor Who

Q: Who played the character of Dexter Morgan in
"Dexter"?
A: Michael C. Hall

Q: What is the name of the vampire slayer in "Buffy
the Vampire Slayer"?
A: Buffy Summers

Q: Which TV show features a chemistry teacher
named Walter White?
A: Breaking Bad

Q: Who played the character of Carrie Bradshaw in
"Sex and the City"?
A: Sarah Jessica Parker

Q: What is the name of the park where the characters
in "Parks and Recreation" work?
A: Pawnee Parks Department

Q: Which TV series features the characters Mulder and
Scully?
A: The X-Files

Q: Who played the character of Dr. Gregory House in
"House"?
A: Hugh Laurie

Q: What is the name of the fictional town in "Twin
Peaks"?
A: Twin Peaks

Q: Which TV show features a serial killer who only
targets other killers?
A: Dexter

Q: Who played the character of Ross Geller in "Friends"?
A: David Schwimmer

Q: What is the name of the fictional law firm in "Suits"?
A: Pearson Hardman

Q: Which TV series features a group of people stranded on a mysterious island?
A: Lost

Q: Who played the character of Sheldon Cooper's roommate Leonard Hofstadter in "The Big Bang Theory"?
A: Johnny Galecki

Q: What is the name of the British series that inspired "The Office"?
A: The Office (UK)

Q: Which TV show features a character named Jack Bauer?
A: 24

Q: Who played the character of Hannah Montana?
A: Miley Cyrus

Q: What is the name of the fictional town in "Riverdale"?
A: Riverdale

Q: Which TV series is based on the Archie Comics characters?
A: Riverdale

Q: Who played the character of Lorelai Gilmore in "Gilmore Girls"?
A: Lauren Graham

Q: What is the name of the hospital in "Grey's Anatomy"?
A: Grey Sloan Memorial Hospital

Q: Which TV show features a character named Eric Cartman?
A: South Park

Q: Who played the character of Don Draper's wife Betty in "Mad Men"?
A: January Jones

Q: What is the name of the fictional town in "Desperate Housewives"?
A: Wisteria Lane

Q: Which TV series features a group of survivors living in a bunker after a nuclear apocalypse?
A: The 100

Q: Who played the character of Peggy Olson in "Mad Men"?
A: Elisabeth Moss

Q: What is the name of the coffeehouse in "Friends"?
A: Central Perk

Q: Which TV show features a high school glee club called New Directions?
A: Glee

Q: Who played the character of Jax Teller in "Sons of Anarchy"?
A: Charlie Hunnam

Q: What is the name of the fictional island in "Lost"?
A: The Island

Q: Which TV series features a character named Meredith Grey?
A: Grey's Anatomy

Q: Who played the character of Walter White's wife Skyler in "Breaking Bad"?
A: Anna Gunn

Q: What is the name of the school in "Stranger Things"?
A: Hawkins Middle School

Q: Which TV show features a character named Leslie Knope?
A: Parks and Recreation

Q: Who played the character of Tyrion Lannister in "Game of Thrones"?
A: Peter Dinklage

Q: What is the name of the fictional hospital in "Scrubs"?
A: Sacred Heart Hospital

Q: Which TV show features a character named Walter White Jr.?
A: Breaking Bad

Q: Who played the character of Olivia Benson in "Law & Order: Special Victims Unit"?
A: Mariska Hargitay

Q: What is the name of the spaceship in "Star Trek: The Next Generation"?
A: USS Enterprise (NCC-1701-D)

Q: Which TV series features a character named Daryl Dixon?
A: The Walking Dead

Q: Who played the character of Piper Chapman in "Orange Is the New Black"?
A: Taylor Schilling

Q: What is the name of the city where "The Wire" is set?
A: Baltimore

Q: Which TV show features a character named Liz Lemon?
A: 30 Rock

Q: Who played the character of Barney Stinson in "How I Met Your Mother"?
A: Neil Patrick Harris

Q: What is the name of the spaceship in "Battlestar Galactica"?
A: Galactica

Q: Which TV series features a character named Walter Bishop?
A: Fringe

Q: Who played the character of Sookie Stackhouse in "True Blood"?
A: Anna Paquin

Q: What is the name of the fictional town in "Stranger Things"?
A: Hawkins

Q: Which TV show features a character named Jessica Jones?
A: Jessica Jones

Q: Who played the character of Philip Jennings in "The Americans"?
A: Matthew Rhys

Q: What is the name of the bar in "Cheers"?
A: Cheers

Q: Which TV series features a character named Carrie Mathison?
A: Homeland

Q: Who played the character of Sherlock Holmes in the TV series "Sherlock"?
A: Benedict Cumberbatch

Q: What is the name of the fictional town in "The Vampire Diaries"?
A: Mystic Falls

Q: Which TV show features a character named Jack Pearson?
A: This Is Us

Q: Who played the character of Peggy Carter in "Agent Carter"?
A: Hayley Atwell

Q: What is the name of the coffee shop in "Gilmore Girls"?
A: Luke's Diner

Q: Which TV series features a character named Richard Castle?
A: Castle

Q: Who played the character of Kara Zor-El in "Supergirl"?
A: Melissa Benoist

Q: What is the name of the spaceship in "The Expanse"?
A: Rocinante

Q: Which TV show features a character named Raymond Reddington?
A: The Blacklist

Q: Who played the character of Dr. John Watson in "Sherlock"?
A: Martin Freeman

Q: What is the name of the high school in "Riverdale"?
A: Riverdale High School

Q: Which TV series features a character named Selina Meyer?
A: Veep

Q: Who played the character of Jessica Day in "New Girl"?
A: Zooey Deschanel

Q: What is the name of the fictional law firm in "Suits"?
A: Pearson Specter Litt

Q: Which TV show features a character named Kara Thrace?
A: Battlestar Galactica

Q: Who played the character of Ragnar Lothbrok in "Vikings"?
A: Travis Fimmel

Q: What is the name of the coffee shop in "Friends"?
A: Central Perk

Q: Which TV series features a character named Walter White Jr.?
A: Breaking Bad

Q: Who played the character of Daenerys Targaryen in "Game of Thrones"?
A: Emilia Clarke

Music Pop Culture Trivia

Pop culture in the music industry is a vibrant tapestry woven with diverse genres, iconic artists, and global trends. From chart-topping hits that dominate airwaves to viral sensations born on social media, music shapes cultural identities and connects people across borders. Artists become cultural icons, influencing fashion, language, and social movements.

Award shows like the Grammys celebrate artistic excellence while showcasing evolving musical styles and performances. Streaming platforms redefine how music is consumed, empowering independent artists and diversifying audiences. Music festivals and concerts provide immersive experiences, uniting fans in shared passion and creating unforgettable moments.

In an era of digital innovation, the music industry continues to evolve, reflecting and shaping the ever-changing landscape of pop culture.

Q: Which artist is known as the "King of Pop"?
A: Michael Jackson

Q: What was the Beatles' first album?
A: Please Please Me

Q: Who sang the 1980 hit "Call Me"?

A: Blondie

Q: Which album by Adele won the Grammy for Album of the Year in 2012?
A: 21

Q: What is the best-selling album of all time?
A: Thriller by Michael Jackson

Q: Who was the lead singer of Queen?
A: Freddie Mercury

Q: Which song by Whitney Houston became the best-selling single by a female artist in history?
A: I Will Always Love You

Q: Which band released the album "Dark Side of the Moon"?
A: Pink Floyd

Q: Who is known as the "Queen of Soul"?
A: Aretha Franklin

Q: Which song by Luis Fonsi and Daddy Yankee became a global hit in 2017?
A: Despacito

Q: Who wrote and performed the song "Imagine"?
A: John Lennon

Q: What is the highest-charting single by Nirvana?
A: Smells Like Teen Spirit

Q: Which artist had a hit with the song "Purple Rain"?
A: Prince

Q: What was the name of the first album released by Beyoncé?
A: Dangerously in Love

Q: Who sang the hit song "Happy" from the "Despicable Me 2" soundtrack?
A: Pharrell Williams

Q: Which band was Freddie Mercury a member of?
A: Queen

Q: What was Elvis Presley's first number-one hit in the United States?
A: Heartbreak Hotel

Q: Which album by Taylor Swift won the Grammy for Album of the Year in 2021?
A: Folklore

Q: Who is known as the "Godfather of Soul"?
A: James Brown

Q: Which band released the album "Nevermind"?
A: Nirvana

Q: Who sang the 2010 hit "Rolling in the Deep"?
A: Adele

Q: What is the name of the first album by The Rolling Stones?
A: The Rolling Stones (England's Newest Hit Makers)

Q: Which song by The Eagles is known for its iconic guitar solo?
A: Hotel California

Q: Who performed the hit song "Like a Prayer"?
A: Madonna

Q: Which artist released the album "Lemonade" in 2016?
A: Beyoncé

Q: Who was the lead singer of The Doors?
A: Jim Morrison

Q: Which song by Ed Sheeran was a major hit in 2017?
A: Shape of You

Q: What was the debut album of the band U2?
A: Boy

Q: Who sang the 1971 hit "What's Going On"?
A: Marvin Gaye

Q: Which artist released the album "FutureSex/LoveSounds"?
A: Justin Timberlake

Q: Who was the drummer for The Beatles?
A: Ringo Starr

Q: Which song by Elton John is often associated with Princess Diana?
A: Candle in the Wind

Q: What is the title of the debut album by Billie Eilish?
A: When We All Fall Asleep, Where Do We Go?

Q: Who sang the 1999 hit "Baby One More Time"?
A: Britney Spears

Q: Which band released the album "Rumours"?
A: Fleetwood Mac

Q: Who is known as the "Material Girl"?
A: Madonna

Q: Which song by The Weeknd spent 90 weeks on the Billboard Hot 100?
A: Blinding Lights

Q: What is the name of the first album by Radiohead?
A: Pablo Honey

Q: Who performed the hit song "Uptown Funk"?
A: Mark Ronson featuring Bruno Mars

Q: Which artist released the album "The Wall"?
A: Pink Floyd

Q: Who sang the 1983 hit "Billie Jean"?
A: Michael Jackson

Q: What was the name of the debut album by Lady Gaga?
A: The Fame

Q: Which song by Bob Dylan became an anthem of the 1960s civil rights movement?
A: Blowin' in the Wind

Q: Who was the lead guitarist for The Jimi Hendrix Experience?
A: Jimi Hendrix

Q: Which band released the album "A Night at the Opera"?

A: Queen

Q: Who sang the 1991 hit "Smells Like Teen Spirit"?
A: Nirvana

Q: What is the title of the debut album by Kendrick
Lamar?
A: Section.80

Q: Which song by Whitney Houston became a
worldwide hit in 1992?
A: I Will Always Love You

Q: Who performed the hit song "Sweet Child O'
Mine"?
A: Guns N' Roses

Q: What was the name of the first album released by
Kanye West?
A: The College Dropout

Q: Which song by Mariah Carey is a popular Christmas
hit?
A: All I Want for Christmas Is You

Q: Who was the lead singer of Nirvana?
A: Kurt Cobain

Q: Which artist released the album "1989" in 2014?
A: Taylor Swift

Q: Who performed the hit song "Bohemian
Rhapsody"?
A: Queen

Q: What is the name of the first album by The Beatles?

A: Please Please Me

Q: Which song by Adele won the Grammy for Record of the Year in 2012?
A: Rolling in the Deep

Q: Who sang the 1978 hit "Stayin' Alive"?
A: Bee Gees

Q: What was the name of David Bowie's alter ego?
A: Ziggy Stardust

Q: Which band released the album "Abbey Road"?
A: The Beatles

Q: Who sang the hit song "All of Me"?
A: John Legend

Q: What was the debut album of The Notorious B.I.G.?
A: Ready to Die

Q: Who performed the song "Superstition"?
A: Stevie Wonder

Q: Which artist released the album "Fearless" in 2008?
A: Taylor Swift

Q: Who sang the 1996 hit "Wannabe"?
A: Spice Girls

Q: What is the title of the debut album by Amy Winehouse?
A: Frank

Q: Who performed the hit song "Hotline Bling"?

A: Drake

Q: Which artist released the album "Thriller"?
A: Michael Jackson

Q: Who sang the 1984 hit "Like a Virgin"?
A: Madonna

Q: What is the name of the first album by Arctic Monkeys?
A: Whatever People Say I Am, That's What I'm Not

Q: Who performed the song "Rolling in the Deep"?
A: Adele

Q: Which band released the album "OK Computer"?
A: Radiohead

Q: Who sang the hit song "Royals"?
A: Lorde

Q: What is the name of the first album by Jay-Z?
A: Reasonable Doubt

Q: Who performed the song "Hey Jude"?
A: The Beatles

Q: Which artist released the album "To Pimp a Butterfly"?
A: Kendrick Lamar

Q: Who sang the 1997 hit "Mmmbop"?
A: Hanson

Q: What is the title of the debut album by Billie Eilish?
A: When We All Fall Asleep, Where Do We Go?

Q: Who performed the hit song "Blurred Lines"?
A: Robin Thicke featuring T.I. and Pharrell

Q: Which artist released the album "Born to Die" in 2012?
A: Lana Del Rey

Q: Who sang the 2003 hit "Crazy in Love"?
A: Beyoncé featuring Jay-Z

Q: What was the name of the first album released by Coldplay?
A: Parachutes

Q: Who performed the hit song "Toxic"?
A: Britney Spears

Q: Which artist released the album "25" in 2015?
A: Adele

Q: Who sang the 2004 hit "Yeah!"?
A: Usher featuring Lil Jon and Ludacris

Q: What is the title of the debut album by The Weeknd?
A: Kiss Land

Q: Who performed the hit song "Lean On"?
A: Major Lazer & DJ Snake featuring MØ

Q: Which artist released the album "good kid, m.A.A.d city"?
A: Kendrick Lamar

Q: Who sang the 2002 hit "Complicated"?

A: Avril Lavigne

Q: What is the name of the first album by Green Day?
A: 39/Smooth

Q: Who performed the hit song "Lose Yourself"?
A: Eminem

Q: Which artist released the album "÷ (Divide)" in 2017?
A: Ed Sheeran

Q: Who sang the 2008 hit "Poker Face"?
A: Lady Gaga

Q: What is the title of the debut album by Cardi B?
A: Invasion of Privacy

Q: Who performed the hit song "Blinding Lights"?
A: The Weeknd

Q: Which artist released the album "thank u, next" in 2019?
A: Ariana Grande

Q: Who sang the 2000 hit "Bye Bye Bye"?
A: NSYNC

Q: What is the name of the first album by Foo Fighters?
A: Foo Fighters

Q: Who performed the hit song "Old Town Road"?
A: Lil Nas X featuring Billy Ray Cyrus

Q: Which artist released the album "Future Nostalgia" in 2020?
A: Dua Lipa

Q: Who sang the 2014 hit "All About That Bass"?
A: Meghan Trainor

Celebrity Pop Culture Trivia

Pop culture's fascination with celebrities revolves around their personas, scandals, and influence across various media platforms. Celebrities become cultural symbols, shaping trends in fashion, lifestyle, and societal norms. Social media amplifies their reach, allowing direct engagement with fans and the public. From red carpet appearances to candid moments captured by paparazzi, celebrity lives are scrutinized and celebrated. Their endorsements drive consumer behavior, while charitable endeavors and activism spotlight social issues.

Reality TV and celebrity gossip magazines further blur the lines between public and private lives, fueling a continuous cycle of intrigue and adoration. In an era of instant access, celebrities navigate fame's highs and lows, contributing to pop culture's ever-evolving narrative.

Q: Which actor played Jack Dawson in "Titanic"?
A: Leonardo DiCaprio

Q: Who is known as the "Queen of Pop"?
A: Madonna

Q: Which actress is famous for her role as Hermione Granger in the "Harry Potter" series?

A: Emma Watson

Q: Who is married to Beyoncé?
A: Jay-Z

Q: Which actor is known for his role as Captain Jack Sparrow in "Pirates of the Caribbean"?
A: Johnny Depp

Q: Who won an Oscar for Best Actor for his role in "The Revenant"?
A: Leonardo DiCaprio

Q: Which singer had a public feud with Taylor Swift that inspired the song "Bad Blood"?
A: Katy Perry

Q: Who is known for her "meat dress" worn at the 2010 MTV Video Music Awards?
A: Lady Gaga

Q: Which actor played Tony Stark/Iron Man in the Marvel Cinematic Universe?
A: Robert Downey Jr.

Q: Who is the youngest self-made billionaire according to Forbes in 2019?
A: Kylie Jenner

Q: Which actress starred as Katniss Everdeen in "The Hunger Games" series?
A: Jennifer Lawrence

Q: Who did Justin Bieber marry in 2018?
A: Hailey Baldwin

Q: Which actor famously said "I'll be back" in "The Terminator"?
A: Arnold Schwarzenegger

Q: Who is known for his role as Wolverine in the "X-Men" series?
A: Hugh Jackman

Q: Which actress played Rachel Green on "Friends"?
A: Jennifer Aniston

Q: Who is the highest-paid female athlete in 2020 according to Forbes?
A: Naomi Osaka

Q: Which actor starred as Neo in "The Matrix" series?
A: Keanu Reeves

Q: Who was the lead singer of the band No Doubt before becoming a solo artist?
A: Gwen Stefani

Q: Which actress is known for her role as Black Widow in the Marvel Cinematic Universe?
A: Scarlett Johansson

Q: Who is the author of the "Harry Potter" series?
A: J.K. Rowling

Q: Which actor is famous for his role as Jack Bauer in "24"?
A: Kiefer Sutherland

Q: Who did Kim Kardashian marry in 2014?
A: Kanye West

Q: Which actor played Frodo Baggins in "The Lord of the Rings" series?
A: Elijah Wood

Q: Who is known as the "Material Girl"?
A: Madonna

Q: Which singer was discovered on YouTube at the age of 13?
A: Justin Bieber

Q: Who played the character of Tony Stark/Iron Man in the Marvel Cinematic Universe?
A: Robert Downey Jr.

Q: Which actress starred in the movie "La La Land" alongside Ryan Gosling?
A: Emma Stone

Q: Who is known for her role as Eleven in the Netflix series "Stranger Things"?
A: Millie Bobby Brown

Q: Which actor voiced the character of Woody in the "Toy Story" series?
A: Tom Hanks

Q: Who is known for her songs "Rolling in the Deep" and "Someone Like You"?
A: Adele

Q: Which actor played the character of Indiana Jones?
A: Harrison Ford

Q: Who is the lead singer of the band Coldplay?
A: Chris Martin

Q: Which actress starred in the film "Legally Blonde"?
A: Reese Witherspoon

Q: Who played the character of Forrest Gump?
A: Tom Hanks

Q: Which singer released the album "Lemonade" in 2016?
A: Beyoncé

Q: Who played the character of Batman in "The Dark Knight" trilogy?
A: Christian Bale

Q: Which actor is known for his roles in "Fight Club" and "Ocean's Eleven"?
A: Brad Pitt

Q: Who is known for her hit single "Hello"?
A: Adele

Q: Which actress starred as Bella Swan in the "Twilight" series?
A: Kristen Stewart

Q: Who is known for his role as Deadpool in the Marvel movies?
A: Ryan Reynolds

Q: Who played the character of Wonder Woman in the 2017 film?
A: Gal Gadot

Q: Which actor starred in "Mission: Impossible" series as Ethan Hunt?

A: Tom Cruise

Q: Who is known for her role as Daenerys Targaryen in "Game of Thrones"?
A: Emilia Clarke

Q: Which actress played the character of Harley Quinn in "Suicide Squad"?
A: Margot Robbie

Q: Who is known for his role as Captain America in the Marvel Cinematic Universe?
A: Chris Evans

Q: Which singer was born with the name Stefani Joanne Angelina Germanotta?
A: Lady Gaga

Q: Who played the character of Jack in "Titanic"?
A: Leonardo DiCaprio

Q: Which actress starred in "The Devil Wears Prada" alongside Meryl Streep?
A: Anne Hathaway

Q: Who is known for her hit song "Bad Romance"?
A: Lady Gaga

Q: Which actor played the character of Tony Stark/Iron Man in the Marvel Cinematic Universe?
A: Robert Downey Jr.

Q: Who starred as the titular character in the "Wonder Woman" movies?
A: Gal Gadot

Q: Which actress played Katniss Everdeen in "The Hunger Games" series?
A: Jennifer Lawrence

Q: Who is the lead singer of Maroon 5?
A: Adam Levine

Q: Which actor played the character of James Bond in "Casino Royale"?
A: Daniel Craig

Q: Who starred as the main character in the TV series "Breaking Bad"?
A: Bryan Cranston

Q: Which actress played the character of Hermione Granger in the "Harry Potter" series?
A: Emma Watson

Q: Who is known for his role as Tony Stark/Iron Man in the Marvel Cinematic Universe?
A: Robert Downey Jr.

Q: Which singer released the hit single "Roar" in 2013?
A: Katy Perry

Q: Who played the character of Captain America in the Marvel Cinematic Universe?
A: Chris Evans

Q: Which actress starred in the TV series "Friends" as Rachel Green?
A: Jennifer Aniston

Q: Who is known for her role as Eleven in "Stranger Things"?

A: Millie Bobby Brown

Q: Which actor starred in the "John Wick" series?
A: Keanu Reeves

Q: Who is known for her hit songs "Rolling in the Deep" and "Someone Like You"?
A: Adele

Q: Which actress played the character of Daenerys Targaryen in "Game of Thrones"?
A: Emilia Clarke

Q: Who is known for his roles in "The Wolf of Wall Street" and "Inception"?
A: Leonardo DiCaprio

Q: Which actor played the character of Thor in the Marvel Cinematic Universe?
A: Chris Hemsworth

Q: Who is known for her role as Katniss Everdeen in "The Hunger Games" series?
A: Jennifer Lawrence

Q: Which singer released the album "Lemonade" in 2016?
A: Beyoncé

Q: Who played the character of Black Widow in the Marvel Cinematic Universe?
A: Scarlett Johansson

Sports Pop Culture Trivia

Pop culture intertwines deeply with sports, elevating athletes to iconic status through remarkable achievements and transcendent moments. From historic championships to record-breaking performances, sports captivate global audiences and inspire collective passion. Athletes become cultural heroes, admired for their skill, resilience, and influence both on and off the field.

Major sporting events like the Olympics and Super Bowl transcend mere competition, becoming spectacles that unify diverse cultures and nations. Social media amplifies athlete endorsements and personal stories, connecting fans intimately with their favorite stars. Sports fashion and lifestyle trends reflect athletes' influence, shaping mainstream culture. In an era of digital media and global connectivity, sports continue to define and redefine pop culture, showcasing human achievement and resilience in the pursuit of greatness.

Q: Who holds the record for the most home runs in a single MLB season?
A: Barry Bonds

Q: Which country won the FIFA World Cup in 2018?
A: France

Q: Who has won the most NBA championships as a player?
A: Bill Russell

Q: Which tennis player has the most Grand Slam titles in men's singles?
A: Rafael Nadal

Q: Who is the only athlete to play in both a Super Bowl and a World Series?
A: Deion Sanders

Q: Which country has won the most Olympic gold medals in history?
A: United States

Q: Who is the fastest man in the world, holding the 100m sprint record?
A: Usain Bolt

Q: Which golfer has won the most major championships?
A: Jack Nicklaus

Q: Who scored the famous "Hand of God" goal in the 1986 FIFA World Cup?
A: Diego Maradona

Q: Which NFL team has the most Super Bowl wins?
A: Pittsburgh Steelers and New England Patriots (tied)

Q: Who is the youngest player to score 10,000 points in the NBA?
A: LeBron James

Q: Which boxer was known as "The Greatest" and "The People's Champion"?
A: Muhammad Ali

Q: Which country won the first FIFA World Cup in 1930?
A: Uruguay

Q: Who is the most decorated Olympian of all time?
A: Michael Phelps

Q: Which NBA player is known as "The Black Mamba"?
A: Kobe Bryant

Q: Who holds the record for the most goals in a single Premier League season?
A: Erling Haaland

Q: Which MLB player is nicknamed "The Sultan of Swat"?
A: Babe Ruth

Q: Who won the women's singles title at Wimbledon in 2021?
A: Ashleigh Barty

Q: Which country has won the most Rugby World Cups?
A: New Zealand

Q: Who is known as "The Great One" in ice hockey?
A: Wayne Gretzky

Q: Which cyclist has won the Tour de France the most times?

A: Lance Armstrong (titles later stripped)

Q: Who scored the winning goal in the 2010 FIFA
World Cup final?
A: Andrés Iniesta

Q: Which tennis player is known as the "King of Clay"?
A: Rafael Nadal

Q: Who is the only person to have won the Heisman
Trophy twice?
A: Archie Griffin

Q: Which female gymnast has won the most Olympic
medals?
A: Larisa Latynina

Q: Who is the all-time leading scorer in the NBA?
A: Kareem Abdul-Jabbar

Q: Which country won the ICC Cricket World Cup in
2019?
A: England

Q: Who holds the record for the most points in a
single NBA game?
A: Wilt Chamberlain

Q: Which soccer player has won the most Ballon d'Or
awards?
A: Lionel Messi

Q: Who is the only athlete to win gold medals in both
the Summer and Winter Olympics?
A: Eddie Eagan

Q: Which NFL quarterback has won the most Super Bowl MVP awards?
A: Tom Brady

Q: Who won the FIFA Women's World Cup in 2019?
A: United States

Q: Which boxer was known as "Iron Mike"?
A: Mike Tyson

Q: Who holds the record for the most goals in NHL history?
A: Wayne Gretzky

Q: Which tennis player won the "Golden Slam" in 1988?
A: Steffi Graf

Q: Who is the all-time top scorer in the UEFA Champions League?
A: Cristiano Ronaldo

Q: Which country has hosted the most Olympic Games?
A: United States

Q: Who was the first female gymnast to score a perfect 10 in the Olympics?
A: Nadia Comăneci

Q: Which MLB team has won the most World Series titles?
A: New York Yankees

Q: Who won the MVP award in the 2020-2021 NBA season?

A: Nikola Jokić

Q: Which soccer player is known as "The Phenomenon"?
A: Ronaldo Nazário

Q: Who was the first African-American to win the Wimbledon singles title?
A: Althea Gibson

Q: Which NFL team went undefeated in the regular season and won the Super Bowl in 1972?
A: Miami Dolphins

Q: Who is the all-time leading scorer in the FIFA World Cup?
A: Miroslav Klose

Q: Which country won the most medals in the 2016 Summer Olympics?
A: United States

Q: Who holds the record for the fastest serve in tennis history?
A: Sam Groth

Q: Which golfer is known as "The Golden Bear"?
A: Jack Nicklaus

Q: Who won the Ballon d'Or in 2021?
A: Lionel Messi

Q: Which team won the NBA championship in 2021?
A: Milwaukee Bucks

Q: Who is the first female driver to win an IndyCar race?
A: Danica Patrick

Q: Which country has won the most FIFA Women's World Cups?
A: United States

Q: Who is the all-time leading scorer in college basketball?
A: Pete Maravich

Q: Which team won the 2018 FIFA World Cup?
A: France

Q: Who holds the record for the most consecutive Wimbledon titles?
A: Roger Federer

Q: Which NFL player is known as "The Refrigerator"?
A: William Perry

Q: Who is the youngest player to win a Grand Slam singles title?
A: Martina Hingis

Q: Which MLB player holds the record for the most career hits?
A: Pete Rose

Q: Who won the MVP award in the 2021-2022 NBA season?
A: Nikola Jokić

Q: Which country has won the most Rugby World Cups?

A: New Zealand

Q: Who is known as "The Greatest" in boxing?
A: Muhammad Ali

Q: Which NFL team has the most Super Bowl appearances?
A: New England Patriots

Q: Who is the first athlete to earn over a billion dollars in career earnings?
A: Tiger Woods

Q: Which soccer player is known as "The Atomic Flea"?
A: Lionel Messi

Q: Who won the Heisman Trophy in 2021?
A: Bryce Young

Q: Which country won the ICC Cricket World Cup in 2011?
A: India

Q: Who is the first female athlete to win a gold medal at the Winter Olympics?
A: Hélène de Pourtalès

Q: Which MLB team has the longest championship drought?
A: Chicago Cubs (until 2016)

Q: Who won the Ballon d'Or in 2022?
A: Karim Benzema

Q: Which tennis player is known for his "tweener" shots?
A: Roger Federer

Q: Who holds the record for the most assists in NBA history?
A: John Stockton

Q: Which country won the FIFA Women's World Cup in 2015?
A: United States

Q: Who is the first gymnast to score a perfect 10 at the Olympics?
A: Nadia Comăneci

Q: Which golfer has won the most PGA Tour events?
A: Sam Snead

Q: Who won the MVP award in the 2022-2023 NBA season?
A: Joel Embiid

Q: Which country has won the most medals in the Winter Olympics?
A: Norway

Q: Who is known as "The Flying Finn" in Formula 1 racing?
A: Mika Häkkinen

Q: Which NFL quarterback has thrown the most touchdown passes in a single season?
A: Peyton Manning

Q: Who won the FIFA Women's World Cup in 1999?

A: United States

Q: Which tennis player has won the most Wimbledon singles titles?
A: Martina Navratilova

Q: Who is the all-time top scorer in the English Premier League?
A: Alan Shearer

Q: Which country hosted the 2008 Summer Olympics?
A: China

Q: Who is the youngest player to score 10,000 points in the NBA?
A: LeBron James

Q: Which MLB player hit the most home runs in a single season?
A: Barry Bonds

Q: Who holds the record for the fastest 100m dash time?
A: Usain Bolt

Q: Which country won the 2014 FIFA World Cup?
A: Germany

Q: Who is known as "The Rocket" in snooker?
A: Ronnie O'Sullivan

Q: Which female soccer player has scored the most international goals?
A: Christine Sinclair

Q: Who won the Heisman Trophy in 2020?

A: DeVonta Smith

Q: Which country has won the most medals in the Summer Olympics?
A: United States

Q: Who is the first African-American head coach to win the Super Bowl?
A: Tony Dungy

Q: Which soccer player has the most appearances in the UEFA Champions League?
A: Iker Casillas

Q: Who holds the record for the most points scored in a single NBA game?
A: Wilt Chamberlain

Q: Which country won the ICC Cricket World Cup in 2007?
A: Australia

Q: Who is known as "The Great One" in ice hockey?
A: Wayne Gretzky

Q: Which tennis player has won the most Grand Slam titles in women's singles?
A: Margaret Court

Q: Who is the all-time leading scorer in the NFL?
A: Adam Vinatieri

Q: Which country won the FIFA Women's World Cup in 2011?
A: Japan

Q: Who holds the record for the most no-hitters in MLB history?
A: Nolan Ryan

Q: Which golfer has won the most Masters tournaments?
A: Jack Nicklaus

Q: Who won the FIFA Men's World Cup in 2022?
A: Argentina

Politics Pop Culture Trivia

Pop culture's intersection with politics showcases a dynamic interplay of leadership, influence, and historical milestones. Elected officials become public figures, their speeches and actions shaping societal discourse and policy agendas. Iconic political moments, from landmark legislation to presidential elections, captivate global attention and reflect societal values and aspirations.

Political campaigns harness media and digital platforms to engage voters, often adopting strategies from entertainment and advertising. Social media amplifies political messages and controversies, allowing for direct interaction with constituents and criticism alike. Political satire and commentary in TV shows and comedy further blur the lines between governance and entertainment, shaping public perception and discourse.

In an era of rapid information dissemination, politics remains a central narrative in pop culture, influencing and reflecting societal norms and aspirations.

Q: Who was the first Vice President of the United States?
A: John Adams

Q: Which British Prime Minister served during World War II?
A: Winston Churchill

Q: Who was the first female Prime Minister of the United Kingdom?
A: Margaret Thatcher

Q: Which U.S. President issued the Emancipation Proclamation?
A: Abraham Lincoln

Q: Who was the Soviet leader during the Cuban Missile Crisis?
A: Nikita Khrushchev

Q: Which Indian leader is known for his nonviolent resistance against British rule?
A: Mahatma Gandhi

Q: Who was the first Chancellor of the Federal Republic of Germany (West Germany) after World War II?
A: Konrad Adenauer

Q: Which South African leader fought against apartheid and became the country's first black president?
A: Nelson Mandela

Q: Who was the U.S. President during the Great Depression and most of World War II?
A: Franklin D. Roosevelt

Q: Who led the Bolshevik Revolution in Russia in 1917?

A: Vladimir Lenin

Q: Who was the longest-reigning British monarch before Queen Elizabeth II?
A: Queen Victoria

Q: Which Chinese leader initiated the Cultural Revolution?
A: Mao Zedong

Q: Who was the first female Prime Minister of India?
A: Indira Gandhi

Q: Which U.S. President resigned due to the Watergate scandal?
A: Richard Nixon

Q: Who was the first democratically elected President of Russia?
A: Boris Yeltsin

Q: Which French leader is known for his role in the French Revolution and the subsequent Reign of Terror?
A: Maximilien Robespierre

Q: Who was the first black president of the United States?
A: Barack Obama

Q: Which Egyptian leader signed the Camp David Accords with Israel?
A: Anwar Sadat

Q: Who was the first Chancellor of the German Empire in 1871?
A: Otto von Bismarck

Q: Which U.S. President was assassinated in Dallas, Texas, in 1963?
A: John F. Kennedy

Q: Who led the Solidarity movement in Poland?
A: Lech Wałęsa

Q: Which British Prime Minister signed the Good Friday Agreement?
A: Tony Blair

Q: Who was the longest-serving Prime Minister of Canada?
A: William Lyon Mackenzie King

Q: Which U.S. President initiated the New Deal programs?
A: Franklin D. Roosevelt

Q: Who was the leader of Iraq during the Gulf War in 1991?
A: Saddam Hussein

Q: Which American civil rights leader delivered the "I Have a Dream" speech?
A: Martin Luther King Jr.

Q: Who was the first woman to serve as U.S. Secretary of State?
A: Madeleine Albright

Q: Which U.S. Supreme Court case declared school segregation unconstitutional?
A: Brown v. Board of Education

Q: Who was the leader of the Cuban Revolution in 1959?
A: Fidel Castro

Q: Which U.S. President authorized the Louisiana Purchase?
A: Thomas Jefferson

Q: Who was the first female Chancellor of Germany?
A: Angela Merkel

Q: Which French leader proclaimed himself Emperor in 1804?
A: Napoleon Bonaparte

Q: Who was the first President of the Republic of Turkey?
A: Mustafa Kemal Atatürk

Q: Which South American revolutionary leader is known as "El Libertador"?
A: Simón Bolívar

Q: Who was the U.S. President during the signing of the Treaty of Versailles?
A: Woodrow Wilson

Q: Which British monarch signed the Magna Carta in 1215?
A: King John

Q: Who was the first Prime Minister of Israel?
A: David Ben-Gurion

Q: Which U.S. President established the Peace Corps?
A: John F. Kennedy

Q: Who led the Khmer Rouge in Cambodia?
A: Pol Pot

Q: Which French king was executed during the French Revolution?
A: Louis XVI

Q: Who was the first President of South Korea?
A: Syngman Rhee

Q: Which British Prime Minister is known for the "Iron Curtain" speech?
A: Winston Churchill

Q: Who was the first female President of Brazil?
A: Dilma Rousseff

Q: Which U.S. President delivered the Gettysburg Address?
A: Abraham Lincoln

Q: Who was the first President of the Fifth French Republic?
A: Charles de Gaulle

Q: Which Indian leader is known for the economic liberalization of the 1990s?
A: P. V. Narasimha Rao

Q: Who was the leader of Libya from 1969 to 2011?
A: Muammar Gaddafi

Q: Which U.S. President was in office during the end of the Cold War?
A: George H. W. Bush

Q: Who was the first female Prime Minister of Pakistan?
A: Benazir Bhutto

Q: Which leader is known for initiating the Perestroika and Glasnost reforms in the Soviet Union?
A: Mikhail Gorbachev

Q: Who was the U.S. President during the signing of the Camp David Accords?
A: Jimmy Carter

Q: Which Chinese leader opened China to foreign investment and economic reform in the late 20th century?
A: Deng Xiaoping

Q: Who was the first President of Indonesia?
A: Sukarno

Q: Which U.S. President signed the Civil Rights Act of 1964?
A: Lyndon B. Johnson

Q: Who was the Prime Minister of the United Kingdom during the Falklands War?
A: Margaret Thatcher

Q: Which South African leader won the Nobel Peace Prize alongside Nelson Mandela?
A: F.W. de Klerk

Q: Who was the leader of the Mexican Revolution that began in 1910?
A: Francisco I. Madero

Q: Which U.S. President issued the Monroe Doctrine?
A: James Monroe

Q: Who was the longest-serving President of France?
A: François Mitterrand

Q: Which Egyptian president was overthrown during the Arab Spring in 2011?
A: Hosni Mubarak

Q: Who was the first Prime Minister of Canada?
A: John A. Macdonald

Q: Which U.S. President initiated the Marshall Plan to rebuild Europe after World War II?
A: Harry S. Truman

Q: Who was the first female President of Argentina?
A: Isabel Perón

Q: Which U.S. President led the country through the majority of the Vietnam War?
A: Lyndon B. Johnson

Q: Who was the leader of the National Fascist Party in Italy?
A: Benito Mussolini

Q: Which Prime Minister of India was assassinated in 1984?
A: Indira Gandhi

Q: Who was the first democratically elected President of South Africa?
A: Nelson Mandela

Q: Which U.S. President signed the Affordable Care Act into law?
A: Barack Obama

Q: Who was the leader of North Korea during the Korean War?
A: Kim Il-sung

Q: Which British Prime Minister signed the Maastricht Treaty, leading to the creation of the European Union?
A: John Major

Q: Who was the first President of the Philippines?
A: Emilio Aguinaldo

Q: Which U.S. President authorized the use of atomic bombs during World War II?
A: Harry S. Truman

Q: Who was the longest-serving leader of Cuba?
A: Fidel Castro

Q: Which South American dictator was overthrown in the Chilean coup of 1973?
A: Salvador Allende

Q: Who was the first African-American Secretary of State of the United States?
A: Colin Powell

Q: Which French President served from 1981 to 1995?
A: François Mitterrand

Q: Who was the first President of independent Kenya?
A: Jomo Kenyatta

Q: Which U.S. President led the country during the first Gulf War?
A: George H. W. Bush

Q: Who was the first female Prime Minister of Israel?
A: Golda Meir

Q: Which Russian Tsar was overthrown during the Russian Revolution of 1917?
A: Nicholas II

Q: Who was the first democratically elected President of South Korea?
A: Syngman Rhee

Q: Which U.S. President was in office during the signing of the Panama Canal Treaty?
A: Jimmy Carter

Q: Who was the first President of post-apartheid South Africa?
A: Nelson Mandela

Q: Which British monarch abdicated the throne in 1936?
A: King Edward VIII

Q: Who was the first President of modern-day Russia?
A: Boris Yeltsin

Q: Which U.S. President is known for the "Fourteen Points" peace plan?
A: Woodrow Wilson

Q: Who was the leader of the Indian National Congress during the Indian independence movement?
A: Jawaharlal Nehru

Q: Which U.S. President signed the Voting Rights Act of 1965?
A: Lyndon B. Johnson

Q: Who was the leader of Nazi Germany during World War II?
A: Adolf Hitler

Q: Which Prime Minister of Japan served the longest uninterrupted term?
A: Shinzo Abe

Q: Who was the first President of the United States to be impeached?
A: Andrew Johnson

Q: Which French Revolution leader became the Emperor of the French?
A: Napoleon Bonaparte

Q: Who was the leader of the Vietnamese Communist Party during the Vietnam War?
A: Ho Chi Minh

Q: Which U.S. President established the Environmental Protection Agency?
A: Richard Nixon

Q: Who was the longest-serving Prime Minister of India?
A: Jawaharlal Nehru

Q: Which British leader is known for the policy of appeasement towards Nazi Germany?
A: Neville Chamberlain

Q: Who was the first President of independent Ghana?
A: Kwame Nkrumah

Q: Which U.S. President was awarded the Nobel Peace Prize in 2009?
A: Barack Obama

Q: Who was the first female President of Chile?
A: Michelle Bachelet

Q: Which leader is known for the Iranian Revolution of 1979?
A: Ayatollah Khomeini

Books and Literature Pop Culture Trivia

Pop culture's relationship with literature and the publishing industry encompasses a rich tapestry of classic works, bestsellers, and evolving trends.

Timeless novels and literary icons continue to inspire adaptations that resonate across generations, shaping popular narratives and cultural conversations. Bestselling books become cultural touchstones, influencing language, fashion, and societal discourse. Book-to-film adaptations bridge literature with visual storytelling, bringing beloved characters and plots to new audiences. Social media platforms and digital publishing democratize access to diverse voices and genres, fostering literary communities and sparking viral book trends. Literary awards celebrate artistic excellence and influence publishing trends, while bookstores and online retailers serve as hubs for cultural exchange and exploration.

In an era of digital innovation and global connectivity, books and literature remain pivotal in shaping and reflecting pop culture's evolving landscape.

Q: Who wrote "Pride and Prejudice"?
A: Jane Austen

Q: Which novel begins with the line, "Call me Ishmael"?
A: Moby-Dick

Q: Who is the author of the "Harry Potter" series?
A: J.K. Rowling

Q: Which dystopian novel features the characters Winston Smith and Big Brother?
A: 1984

Q: Who wrote "To Kill a Mockingbird"?
A: Harper Lee

Q: What is the name of the kingdom in C.S. Lewis's "The Chronicles of Narnia"?
A: Narnia

Q: Who is the protagonist of "The Great Gatsby"?
A: Jay Gatsby

Q: Who wrote "One Hundred Years of Solitude"?
A: Gabriel García Márquez

Q: Which novel features the character Holden Caulfield?
A: The Catcher in the Rye

Q: Who wrote "The Hobbit"?
A: J.R.R. Tolkien

Q: Which classic novel features the character Atticus Finch?
A: To Kill a Mockingbird

Q: Who is the author of "Brave New World"?

A: Aldous Huxley

Q: What is the title of the first book in the "A Song of Ice and Fire" series by George R.R. Martin?
A: A Game of Thrones

Q: Who wrote "The Catcher in the Rye"?
A: J.D. Salinger

Q: Which novel begins with the line, "It was the best of times, it was the worst of times"?
A: A Tale of Two Cities

Q: Who is the author of "The Handmaid's Tale"?
A: Margaret Atwood

Q: Which character in "The Lord of the Rings" is known as the Ring-bearer?
A: Frodo Baggins

Q: Who wrote "The Picture of Dorian Gray"?
A: Oscar Wilde

Q: Which novel features the character Elizabeth Bennet?
A: Pride and Prejudice

Q: Who is the author of "Crime and Punishment"?
A: Fyodor Dostoevsky

Q: What is the title of the first book in the "Harry Potter" series?
A: Harry Potter and the Sorcerer's Stone

Q: Who wrote "The Grapes of Wrath"?
A: John Steinbeck

Q: Which novel is set in the fictional town of Maycomb, Alabama?
A: To Kill a Mockingbird

Q: Who is the author of "The Old Man and the Sea"?
A: Ernest Hemingway

Q: Which novel features the character Scout Finch?
A: To Kill a Mockingbird

Q: Who wrote "Jane Eyre"?
A: Charlotte Brontë

Q: Which novel is set on the fictional island of Utopia?
A: Utopia

Q: Who is the author of "The Catch-22"?
A: Joseph Heller

Q: Which novel features the character Sherlock Holmes?
A: A Study in Scarlet (and other stories)

Q: Who wrote "Wuthering Heights"?
A: Emily Brontë

Q: Which novel begins with the line, "All happy families are alike; each unhappy family is unhappy in its own way"?
A: Anna Karenina

Q: Who is the author of "Frankenstein"?
A: Mary Shelley

Q: Which novel features the character Huckleberry Finn?
A: The Adventures of Huckleberry Finn

Q: Who wrote "The Scarlet Letter"?
A: Nathaniel Hawthorne

Q: Which novel is set in the fictional country of Oceania?
A: 1984

Q: Who is the author of "Moby-Dick"?
A: Herman Melville

Q: Which novel features the character Anna Karenina?
A: Anna Karenina

Q: Who wrote "The Alchemist"?
A: Paulo Coelho

Q: Which novel begins with the line, "It was a bright cold day in April, and the clocks were striking thirteen"?
A: 1984

Q: Who is the author of "War and Peace"?
A: Leo Tolstoy

Q: Which novel features the character Bilbo Baggins?
A: The Hobbit

Q: Who wrote "Great Expectations"?
A: Charles Dickens

Q: Which novel is set in the fictional town of West Egg?
A: The Great Gatsby

Q: Who is the author of "The Bell Jar"?
A: Sylvia Plath

Q: Which novel features the character Victor Frankenstein?
A: Frankenstein

Q: Who wrote "The Kite Runner"?
A: Khaled Hosseini

Q: Which novel is set in the fictional kingdom of Westeros?
A: A Game of Thrones

Q: Who is the author of "The Sun Also Rises"?
A: Ernest Hemingway

Q: Which novel features the character Katniss Everdeen?
A: The Hunger Games

Q: Who wrote "The Road"?
A: Cormac McCarthy

Q: Which novel begins with the line, "In a hole in the ground there lived a hobbit"?
A: The Hobbit

Q: Who is the author of "Beloved"?
A: Toni Morrison

Q: Which novel features the character Holden Caulfield?
A: The Catcher in the Rye

Q: Who wrote "The Name of the Rose"?
A: Umberto Eco

Q: Which novel is set on the fictional island of Pala?
A: Island

Q: Who is the author of "The Count of Monte Cristo"?
A: Alexandre Dumas

Q: Which novel features the character Lisbeth
Salander?
A: The Girl with the Dragon Tattoo

Q: Who wrote "The Secret Garden"?
A: Frances Hodgson Burnett

Q: Which novel begins with the line, "Marley was dead:
to begin with"?
A: A Christmas Carol

Q: Who is the author of "The Brothers Karamazov"?
A: Fyodor Dostoevsky

Q: Which novel features the character Jay Gatsby?
A: The Great Gatsby

Q: Who wrote "The Book Thief"?
A: Markus Zusak

Q: Which novel is set in the fictional town of
Middlemarch?
A: Middlemarch

Q: Who is the author of "Life of Pi"?
A: Yann Martel

Q: Which novel features the character Scarlett O'Hara?
A: Gone with the Wind

Q: Who wrote "Dracula"?
A: Bram Stoker

Q: Which novel begins with the line, "All children, except one, grow up"?
A: Peter Pan

Q: Who is the author of "The God of Small Things"?
A: Arundhati Roy

Q: Which novel features the character Pip?
A: Great Expectations

Q: Who wrote "The Shining"?
A: Stephen King

Q: Which novel begins with the line, "It was love at first sight"?
A: Catch-22

Q: Who is the author of "The Lovely Bones"?
A: Alice Sebold

Q: Which novel features the character Daisy Buchanan?
A: The Great Gatsby

Q: Who wrote "The Da Vinci Code"?
A: Dan Brown

Q: Which novel is set in the fictional town of Derry, Maine?
A: It

Q: Who is the author of "The Fault in Our Stars"?
A: John Green

Q: Which novel features the character Sam Spade?
A: The Maltese Falcon

Q: Who wrote "The Hitchhiker's Guide to the Galaxy"?
A: Douglas Adams

Q: Which novel begins with the line, "It was a pleasure to burn"?
A: Fahrenheit 451

Q: Who is the author of "The Joy Luck Club"?
A: Amy Tan

Q: Which novel features the character Ignatius J. Reilly?
A: A Confederacy of Dunces

Q: Who wrote "The Road to Wigan Pier"?
A: George Orwell

Q: Which novel is set in the fictional town of Winesburg, Ohio?
A: Winesburg, Ohio

Q: Who is the author of "Slaughterhouse-Five"?
A: Kurt Vonnegut

Q: Which novel features the character Lisbeth Salander?
A: The Girl with the Dragon Tattoo

Q: Who wrote "The Color Purple"?
A: Alice Walker

Q: Which novel begins with the line, "Happy families are all alike; every unhappy family is unhappy in its own way"?
A: Anna Karenina

Q: Who is the author of "Infinite Jest"?
A: David Foster Wallace

Q: Which novel features the character Guy Montag?
A: Fahrenheit 451

Q: Who wrote "The Outsiders"?
A: S.E. Hinton

Q: Which novel is set in the fictional country of Gilead?
A: The Handmaid's Tale

Q: Who is the author of "White Teeth"?
A: Zadie Smith

Q: Which novel features the character Christian Grey?
A: Fifty Shades of Grey

Q: Who wrote "American Gods"?
A: Neil Gaiman

Q: Which novel begins with the line, "The sky above the port was the color of television, tuned to a dead channel"?
A: Neuromancer

Q: Who is the author of "The Goldfinch"?
A: Donna Tartt

Q: Which novel features the character Patrick Bateman?
A: American Psycho

Q: Who wrote "The Brief Wondrous Life of Oscar Wao"?
A: Junot Díaz

Q: Which novel begins with the line, "Mr. and Mrs. Dursley, of number four, Privet Drive, were proud to say that they were perfectly normal, thank you very much"?
A: Harry Potter and the Sorcerer's Stone

Q: Who is the author of "The Shadow of the Wind"?
A: Carlos Ruiz Zafón

Video Games Pop Culture Trivia

Pop culture's fascination with video games has transformed the industry into a powerhouse of creativity, innovation, and community. From iconic characters like Mario and Lara Croft to blockbuster franchises such as Pokémon and Call of Duty, games have become cultural touchstones.

Video game narratives blend storytelling with interactive gameplay, offering immersive experiences that resonate with diverse audiences worldwide. Esports tournaments elevate gaming to competitive spectacles, attracting millions of viewers and inspiring professional careers. Social media platforms and streaming services amplify game culture, fostering communities, memes, and viral trends.

The gaming industry's evolution from arcade cabinets to virtual reality reflects technological advancements and societal shifts, influencing entertainment, fashion, and even education. As gaming continues to innovate and expand, it remains a defining force in shaping contemporary pop culture.

Q: What is the best-selling video game of all time?
A: Minecraft

Q: In which year was the original "Super Mario Bros."
released?
A: 1985

Q: What is the name of the main character in "The
Legend of Zelda" series?
A: Link

Q: Which company developed the game "Fortnite"?
A: Epic Games

Q: What is the highest-grossing arcade game of all time?
A: Pac-Man

Q: Which video game series features the character
Master Chief?
A: Halo

Q: What is the fictional setting of the "Fallout" series
called?
A: The Wasteland

Q: Who is the main antagonist in "Half-Life 2"?
A: Dr. Wallace Breen

Q: What is the name of the first Pokémon game
released in North America?
A: Pokémon Red and Blue

Q: Which game is known for the phrase "Finish Him"?
A: Mortal Kombat

Q: What is the primary currency in "The Legend of
Zelda" series?
A: Rupees

Q: Who is the creator of the "Metal Gear" series?
A: Hideo Kojima

Q: In which game do players explore the island of Yara to overthrow a dictator?
A: Far Cry 6

Q: Which company developed the "Dark Souls" series?
A: FromSoftware

Q: What is the main objective in "Among Us"?
A: To complete tasks or identify the impostors

Q: What year was the original "Sonic the Hedgehog" released?
A: 1991

Q: Which game features the character Kratos, the God of War?
A: God of War

Q: What is the primary setting of the "Assassin's Creed" series?
A: Historical periods and locations

Q: In which game do players control a character named Geralt of Rivia?
A: The Witcher 3: Wild Hunt

Q: What is the name of the princess that Mario often rescues?
A: Princess Peach

Q: Which game features the "Vault-Tec Assisted Targeting System" (V.A.T.S.)?
A: Fallout

Q: What is the main character's profession in "BioShock"?
A: Private investigator

Q: What game is known for its phrase "The cake is a lie"?
A: Portal

Q: Who is the main antagonist in the "Resident Evil" series?
A: Albert Wesker

Q: What is the name of the fictional world in "The Elder Scrolls V: Skyrim"?
A: Tamriel

Q: Which game features a post-apocalyptic world where robots resemble animals?
A: Horizon Zero Dawn

Q: Who is the main character in the "Tomb Raider" series?
A: Lara Croft

Q: What is the name of the kingdom in "Super Mario 64"?
A: Mushroom Kingdom

Q: Which game series features a character named Dante who battles demons?
A: Devil May Cry

Q: What is the name of the primary weapon in "Halo"?
A: Energy Sword

Q: In which game do players explore the underwater city of Rapture?
A: BioShock

Q: Who is the protagonist of "Red Dead Redemption 2"?
A: Arthur Morgan

Q: What game popularized the battle royale genre?
A: PUBG: PlayerUnknown's Battlegrounds

Q: Which game features the character Solid Snake?
A: Metal Gear Solid

Q: What is the name of the town where "Silent Hill" is set?
A: Silent Hill

Q: Who is the creator of the "Super Smash Bros." series?
A: Masahiro Sakurai

Q: What is the main character's name in "The Last of Us"?
A: Joel (and Ellie in Part II)

Q: Which game features a city called Vice City?
A: Grand Theft Auto: Vice City

Q: What is the name of the protagonist in "Assassin's Creed II"?
A: Ezio Auditore da Firenze

Q: In which game do players collect and craft items to survive on an alien planet called 4546B?
A: Subnautica

Q: What year was the Nintendo 64 released?
A: 1996

Q: Which game series features the character Gordon Freeman?
A: Half-Life

Q: What is the name of the main city in "The Elder Scrolls V: Skyrim"?
A: Whiterun

Q: Which game features the phrase "War. War never changes"?
A: Fallout

Q: Who is the main character in the "Mass Effect" series?
A: Commander Shepard

Q: In which game do players control a young boy named Link?
A: The Legend of Zelda

Q: What is the primary mode of transportation in "Death Stranding"?
A: Walking and using a BB (Bridge Baby)

Q: Which game features a character named Cloud Strife?
A: Final Fantasy VII

Q: Who is the main character in "BioShock Infinite"?
A: Booker DeWitt

Q: What game features the character Arthur Morgan?

A: Red Dead Redemption 2

Q: Which game series includes the location Raccoon City?
A: Resident Evil

Q: What is the name of the protagonist in "The Legend of Zelda: Breath of the Wild"?
A: Link

Q: Which game is known for its iconic phrase "It's dangerous to go alone! Take this."?
A: The Legend of Zelda

Q: Who is the main character in the "Metroid" series?
A: Samus Aran

Q: What is the name of the main character in "God of War"?
A: Kratos

Q: In which game do players explore the land of Hyrule?
A: The Legend of Zelda

Q: Who is the main antagonist in "Far Cry 3"?
A: Vaas Montenegro

Q: Which game features the character Aloy?
A: Horizon Zero Dawn

Q: What is the name of the protagonist in "The Witcher" series?
A: Geralt of Rivia

Q: Which game features the location Columbia, a floating city?
A: BioShock Infinite

Q: Who is the main character in "Final Fantasy X"?
A: Tidus

Q: What is the name of the open-world game developed by Rockstar Games that features cowboys?
A: Red Dead Redemption

Q: Which game series features the character Nathan Drake?
A: Uncharted

Q: What is the name of the protagonist in "Assassin's Creed Odyssey"?
A: Alexios or Kassandra

Q: In which game do players control a knight exploring the kingdom of Hallownest?
A: Hollow Knight

Q: What is the name of the main character in "Control"?
A: Jesse Faden

Q: Which game series features a haunted animatronic restaurant?
A: Five Nights at Freddy's

Q: Who is the main character in "The Last of Us Part II"?
A: Ellie

Q: Which game features a character named Arthur Morgan?
A: Red Dead Redemption 2

Q: What is the name of the city where "Cyberpunk 2077" is set?
A: Night City

Q: Which game features the character Solid Snake?
A: Metal Gear Solid

Q: Who is the main character in the "Bayonetta" series?
A: Bayonetta

Q: In which game do players control a character named Ethan Winters?
A: Resident Evil 7: Biohazard

Q: What is the name of the main character in "Sekiro: Shadows Die Twice"?
A: Wolf (Sekiro)

Q: Which game features the character Sora and his friends Donald and Goofy?
A: Kingdom Hearts

Q: Who is the protagonist of the "BioShock" series?
A: Jack (BioShock), Subject Delta (BioShock 2), and Booker DeWitt (BioShock Infinite)

Q: What is the name of the main character in "Persona 5"?
A: Joker

Q: Which game features a city called New Bordeaux?
A: Mafia III

Q: Who is the main character in "Bloodborne"?
A: The Hunter

Q: In which game do players control a character named Samus Aran?
A: Metroid

Q: Which game features a world called Tamriel?
A: The Elder Scrolls series

Q: Who is the main character in the "Half-Life" series?
A: Gordon Freeman

Q: What is the name of the protagonist in "Nier: Automata"?
A: 2B

Q: Which game series includes the location Vice City?
A: Grand Theft Auto

Q: Who is the main character in "The Legend of Zelda: Ocarina of Time"?
A: Link

Q: What is the name of the main character in "Celeste"?
A: Madeline

Q: Which game features the phrase "War never changes"?
A: Fallout

Q: Who is the protagonist in the "Far Cry 4"?
A: Ajay Ghale

Q: In which game do players explore the underwater city of Rapture?
A: BioShock

Q: What is the name of the protagonist in "Dead Space"?
A: Isaac Clarke

Q: Which game features the character Ezio Auditore da Firenze?
A: Assassin's Creed II

Q: Who is the main character in "Death Stranding"?
A: Sam Porter Bridges

Q: What is the name of the protagonist in "Dishonored"?
A: Corvo Attano

Q: Which game series features the character Big Boss?
A: Metal Gear

Q: Who is the main character in "Control"?
A: Jesse Faden

Q: What is the name of the protagonist in "Final Fantasy XV"?
A: Noctis Lucis Caelum

Q: Which game features the character Commander Shepard?
A: Mass Effect

Q: Who is the main character in "Persona 4"?
A: Yu Narukami

Q: In which game do players control a knight
exploring the kingdom of Hallownest?
A: Hollow Knight

Q: Who is the protagonist of "The Witcher 3: Wild
Hunt"?
A: Geralt of Rivia

Memes and Internet Pop Culture Trivia

Pop culture's fascination with memes and internet viral stars showcases a dynamic landscape of humor, creativity, and social commentary.

Memes, often combining images and text, spread rapidly across social media platforms, reflecting and satirizing current events, trends, and pop culture phenomena. Internet viral stars, from "Keyboard Cat" to influencers like "Grumpy Cat," captivate audiences with their quirky personalities and unique talents, becoming cultural icons overnight.

These digital phenomena not only entertain but also shape public discourse and online communities, demonstrating the power of humor and relatability in connecting people across the globe.

Q: What is the name of the cat famous for its grumpy expression?
A: Grumpy Cat

Q: Which meme features a young girl smiling in front of a burning house?
A: Disaster Girl

Q: What is the name of the dancing baby that became one of the earliest internet memes?

A: Baby Cha-Cha-Cha or Dancing Baby

Q: Which meme features a distracted boyfriend looking at another woman?
A: Distracted Boyfriend

Q: What phrase did the internet cat "Nyan Cat" repeatedly meow?
A: "Nyan" (Japanese onomatopoeia for a cat's meow)

Q: Who is the star of the "Leave Britney Alone!" viral video?
A: Chris Crocker

Q: Which meme involves a frog sitting on a unicycle?
A: Dat Boi

Q: What is the name of the Shiba Inu dog that is often associated with the "Doge" meme?
A: Kabosu

Q: Which meme features a man running while repeatedly saying "They are taking the hobbits to Isengard"?
A: Taking the Hobbits to Isengard

Q: What is the term for fake news articles that claim absurd or unbelievable events?
A: Clickbait

Q: Who is the "Overly Attached Girlfriend" based on?
A: Laina Morris

Q: Which meme features a young boy flexing his bicep with a determined expression?
A: Success Kid

Q: What phrase is often associated with the image of a man raising his hand while sitting in a classroom?
A: "First World Problems"

Q: Which internet personality is known for the catchphrase "Ain't nobody got time for that"?
A: Sweet Brown

Q: What is the name of the internet sensation that remixed a news clip into the song "Bed Intruder"?
A: Antoine Dodson

Q: Which meme involves a skeleton on a computer with the caption "Still waiting"?
A: "Waiting Skeleton"

Q: What is the name of the meme featuring a confused woman surrounded by mathematical equations?
A: Confused Math Lady

Q: Which meme features a character named Pepe the Frog?
A: Pepe

Q: What is the phrase associated with the Success Kid meme?
A: "Success!"

Q: Who is the star of the "Charlie Bit My Finger" video?
A: Charlie and Harry Davies-Carr

Q: Which meme features a woman yelling at a confused-looking cat?
A: Woman Yelling at a Cat

Q: What phrase became popular after the rapper Drake used it in his song "Hotline Bling"?
A: "You used to call me on my cell phone"

Q: Who is the internet personality known for their "Friday" music video?
A: Rebecca Black

Q: Which meme involves a stock photo of a man looking at another woman while his girlfriend looks on angrily?
A: Distracted Boyfriend

Q: What is the name of the social media challenge where people pour ice water over their heads?
A: Ice Bucket Challenge

Q: Which internet personality is known for his "Let's Play" videos on YouTube?
A: PewDiePie

Q: What is the name of the meme involving a SpongeBob character mocking a phrase?
A: Mocking SpongeBob

Q: Which meme features a man pointing at his head as if having a smart idea?
A: Roll Safe

Q: Who is the internet sensation known for his catchphrase "Damn, Daniel!"?
A: Daniel Lara

Q: What is the name of the viral challenge where people pose as mannequins?

A: Mannequin Challenge

Q: Which meme features a series of screenshots from a music video of a man singing "What is love?"
A: Haddaway's "What is Love?"

Q: What is the name of the viral sensation who sang "Chocolate Rain"?
A: Tay Zonday

Q: Which internet challenge involves people performing a dance to the song "Harlem Shake"?
A: Harlem Shake Challenge

Q: What is the name of the YouTube series where people review bad movies in a humorous way?
A: CinemaSins

Q: Which meme features a dog sitting in a burning room saying "This is fine"?
A: This is Fine Dog

Q: What is the name of the viral dance challenge that involves the song "In My Feelings" by Drake?
A: Kiki Challenge

Q: Who is the internet personality known for her "My Immortal" fanfiction?
A: Tara Gilesbie (though the true identity remains debated)

Q: Which meme features a man blinking in disbelief?
A: Blinking White Guy

Q: What is the name of the viral video where a man dramatically turns his head to reveal a red curtain?

A: Dramatic Chipmunk

Q: Which internet personality is known for the catchphrase "I like turtles"?
A: Jonathan Ware

Q: What is the name of the video game character often associated with the phrase "Do a barrel roll"?
A: Peppy Hare from Star Fox

Q: Which meme features a cat wearing a Pop-Tart body flying through space?
A: Nyan Cat

Q: What is the name of the internet challenge where people lie face down in unusual locations?
A: Planking

Q: Who is the star of the viral video "Double Rainbow"?
A: Paul "Bear" Vasquez

Q: Which meme involves a toddler with a clenched fist and a determined look on his face?
A: Success Kid

Q: What is the name of the viral video featuring a baby laughing hysterically at ripping paper?
A: Laughing Baby

Q: Which meme features an image of a velociraptor contemplating philosophical questions?
A: Philosoraptor

Q: Who is the internet personality known for his "Chocolate Rain" song?

A: Tay Zonday

Q: What is the name of the meme where a child makes a skeptical face while holding a drink?
A: Skeptical Third World Kid

Q: Which meme features a dog saying "Such wow" and "Much amaze"?
A: Doge

Q: Who is the internet personality known for the video "Leave Britney Alone"?
A: Chris Crocker

Q: What is the name of the viral trend where people dance to the song "Juju on That Beat"?
A: TZ Anthem Challenge

Q: Which meme features a character from "The Simpsons" walking backwards into a hedge?
A: Homer Simpson Backing Into Bushes

Q: What is the name of the viral dance challenge where people freeze in place?
A: Mannequin Challenge

Q: Which meme features a character from the TV show "Arthur" with a clenched fist?
A: Arthur's Fist

Q: What is the name of the internet personality known for his "Hide Yo Kids, Hide Yo Wife" interview?
A: Antoine Dodson

Q: Which meme features a cat with captions written in broken English?

A: LOLcats

Q: What is the name of the viral trend where people flip bottles and try to land them upright?
A: Bottle Flip Challenge

Q: Which internet personality is known for the catchphrase "It's Wednesday, my dudes"?
A: Jimmy Here

Q: What is the name of the viral video where a man yells "Why you always lying?"
A: Nicholas Fraser

Q: Which meme involves a photo of a couple walking hand-in-hand with the man looking back at another woman?
A: Distracted Boyfriend

Q: What is the name of the internet sensation known for the "Grape Stomping Lady" video?
A: Melissa Sander

Q: Which meme features a cat in a formal pose with the caption "I should buy a boat"?
A: Business Cat

Q: What is the name of the viral challenge where people perform a dance to the song "Juju on That Beat"?
A: TZ Anthem Challenge

Q: Which meme features a boy with a clenched fist and a determined look on his face?
A: Success Kid

Q: What is the name of the viral sensation who remixed a news clip into the song "Bed Intruder"?
A: Antoine Dodson

Q: Which meme features an image of a velociraptor contemplating philosophical questions?
A: Philosoraptor

Q: What is the name of the internet trend where people pose as mannequins?
A: Mannequin Challenge

Q: Which meme involves a photo of a man blinking in disbelief?
A: Blinking White Guy

Q: What is the name of the viral video where a man dramatically turns his head to reveal a red curtain?
A: Dramatic Chipmunk

Q: Which internet personality is known for his "Hide Yo Kids, Hide Yo Wife" interview?
A: Antoine Dodson

Q: What is the name of the internet trend where people lie face down in unusual locations?
A: Planking

Q: Which meme features a cat saying "Such wow" and "Much amaze"?
A: Doge

Q: What is the name of the viral video featuring a baby laughing hysterically at ripping paper?
A: Laughing Baby

Q: Which meme features a character from "The Simpsons" walking backwards into a hedge?
A: Homer Simpson Backing Into Bushes

Q: What is the name of the internet personality known for his "Let's Play" videos on YouTube?
A: PewDiePie

Q: Which meme features a character from the TV show "Arthur" with a clenched fist?
A: Arthur's Fist

Q: What is the name of the viral trend where people flip bottles and try to land them upright?
A: Bottle Flip Challenge

Q: Which internet personality is known for the catchphrase "It's Wednesday, my dudes"?
A: Jimmy Here

Q: What is the name of the viral video where a man yells "Why you always lying?"
A: Nicholas Fraser

Q: Which meme features a cat in a formal pose with the caption "I should buy a boat"?
A: Business Cat

Q: What is the name of the viral sensation known for the "Grape Stomping Lady" video?
A: Melissa Sander

Q: Which meme features a dog sitting in a burning room saying "This is fine"?
A: This is Fine Dog

Q: What is the name of the viral video where a man dramatically turns his head to reveal a red curtain?
A: Dramatic Chipmunk

Q: Which meme features a young boy flexing his bicep with a determined expression?
A: Success Kid

Q: What is the name of the internet personality known for the "Double Rainbow" video?
A: Paul "Bear" Vasquez

Q: Which meme features a character named Pepe the Frog?
A: Pepe

Q: What is the name of the viral sensation who remixed a news clip into the song "Bed Intruder"?
A: Antoine Dodson

Q: Which meme features a cat wearing a Pop-Tart body flying through space?
A: Nyan Cat

Q: What is the name of the internet trend where people pose as mannequins?
A: Mannequin Challenge

Q: Which meme features a dog saying "Such wow" and "Much amaze"?
A: Doge

Q: What is the name of the viral video featuring a baby laughing hysterically at ripping paper?
A: Laughing Baby

Q: Which meme features a character from "The Simpsons" walking backwards into a hedge?
A: Homer Simpson Backing Into Bushes

Q: What is the name of the viral video where a man yells "Why you always lying?"
A: Nicholas Fraser

Q: Which meme features a cat in a formal pose with the caption "I should buy a boat"?
A: Business Cat

Q: What is the name of the viral sensation known for the "Grape Stomping Lady" video?
A: Melissa Sander

Q: Which meme features a dog sitting in a burning room saying "This is fine"?
A: This is Fine Dog

Q: What is the name of the internet personality known for the "Double Rainbow" video?
A: Paul "Bear" Vasquez

Q: Which meme features a character named Pepe the Frog?
A: Pepe

Q: What is the name of the viral sensation who remixed a news clip into the song "Bed Intruder"?
A: Antoine Dodson

Q: What is the name of the viral video where a man dramatically turns his head to reveal a red curtain?
A: Dramatic Chipmunk

Q: Which meme features a young boy flexing his bicep with a determined expression?
A: Success Kid

Q: What is the name of the internet personality known for the "Double Rainbow" video?
A: Paul "Bear" Vasquez

Q: Which meme features a character named Pepe the Frog?
A: Pepe

Q: What is the name of the viral sensation who remixed a news clip into the song "Bed Intruder"?
A: Antoine Dodson

Q: Which meme features a cat wearing a Pop-Tart body flying through space?
A: Nyan Cat

Q: What is the name of the internet trend where people pose as mannequins?
A: Mannequin Challenge

Q: Which meme features a dog saying "Such wow" and "Much amaze"?
A: Doge

Q: What is the name of the viral video featuring a baby laughing hysterically at ripping paper?
A: Laughing Baby

Q: Which meme features a character from "The Simpsons" walking backwards into a hedge?
A: Homer Simpson Backing Into Bushes

Q: What is the name of the viral video where a man yells "Why you always lying?"
A: Nicholas Fraser

Q: Which meme features a cat in a formal pose with the caption "I should buy a boat"?
A: Business Cat

Q: What is the name of the viral sensation known for the "Grape Stomping Lady" video?
A: Melissa Sander

Q: Which meme features a dog sitting in a burning room saying "This is fine"?
A: This is Fine Dog

Q: What is the name of the internet personality known for the "Double Rainbow" video?
A: Paul "Bear" Vasquez

Q: Which meme features a character named Pepe the Frog?
A: Pepe

Q: What is the name of the viral sensation who remixed a news clip into the song "Bed Intruder"?
A: Antoine Dodson

Award Shows Pop Culture Trivia

Pop culture's fascination with Hollywood award shows centers on glamour, prestige, and artistic recognition.

Events like the Oscars, Golden Globes, and Emmys celebrate excellence in film and television, drawing global attention to stars, directors, and creators. These ceremonies set fashion trends, generate memorable speeches, and spark cultural conversations about diversity, inclusion, and industry trends. Award winners become cultural icons, influencing future projects and shaping public perception of entertainment.

The shows themselves are televised spectacles, blending entertainment with industry accolades, and highlighting the intersection of artistry and celebrity in contemporary pop culture.

Q: Which film won the Best Picture Oscar in 2020?
A: Parasite

Q: Who won the Grammy Award for Album of the Year in 2021?
A: Taylor Swift for "Folklore"

Q: Which actor famously declared "You like me, right now, you like me!" in their Oscar acceptance speech?

A: Sally Field

Q: Who won the Best Director Oscar for "The Shape of Water" in 2018?
A: Guillermo del Toro

Q: Which artist holds the record for the most Grammy wins in history?
A: Beyoncé

Q: What film won the Best Picture Oscar in 1994?
A: Forrest Gump

Q: Who was the first woman to win the Best Director Oscar?
A: Kathryn Bigelow for "The Hurt Locker"

Q: Which song won the Grammy for Record of the Year in 2019?
A: "This Is America" by Childish Gambino

Q: Who won the Oscar for Best Actor in 2021?
A: Anthony Hopkins for "The Father"

Q: Which TV show has won the most Emmy Awards for Outstanding Drama Series?
A: Game of Thrones

Q: Who gave a memorable acceptance speech at the Oscars by signing to the audience in 1987?
A: Marlee Matlin

Q: Which film won the first-ever Best Picture Oscar in 1929?
A: Wings

Q: Who won the Grammy for Best New Artist in 2020?
A: Billie Eilish

Q: Which director has won the most Best Director Oscars?
A: John Ford

Q: What movie won the Best Animated Feature Oscar in 2020?
A: Toy Story 4

Q: Who famously said, "I'm king of the world!" during their Oscar acceptance speech?
A: James Cameron

Q: Which artist won the Grammy for Song of the Year in 2021?
A: H.E.R. for "I Can't Breathe"

Q: What film won the Best Picture Oscar in 2019?
A: Green Book

Q: Who won the Emmy for Outstanding Lead Actor in a Drama Series in 2020?
A: Jeremy Strong for "Succession"

Q: Which actress made headlines by performing a striptease while accepting an MTV Movie Award in 1993?
A: Rose McGowan

Q: What film won the Best Picture Oscar in 2016, after the wrong film was initially announced?
A: Moonlight

Q: Who won the Grammy for Best Pop Solo
Performance in 2021?
A: Harry Styles for "Watermelon Sugar"

Q: Which actor received a standing ovation at the
Oscars for winning Best Actor posthumously in 2009?
A: Heath Ledger for "The Dark Knight"

Q: What TV show won the Emmy for Outstanding
Comedy Series in 2020?
A: Schitt's Creek

Q: Who gave a memorable Golden Globe speech in
2020 by calling out Hollywood's hypocrisy?
A: Ricky Gervais

Q: Which film won the Best Picture Oscar in 2001?
A: Gladiator

Q: Who won the Grammy for Album of the Year in
2017?
A: Adele for "25"

Q: What actor has won the most Oscars for acting?
A: Katharine Hepburn

Q: Which film won the Best Foreign Language Film
Oscar in 2019?
A: Roma

Q: Who won the Emmy for Outstanding Lead Actress
in a Drama Series in 2018?
A: Claire Foy for "The Crown"

Q: What artist made headlines by wearing a meat dress
to the MTV Video Music Awards in 2010?

A: Lady Gaga

Q: Which film won the Best Picture Oscar in 1998?
A: Titanic

Q: Who won the Grammy for Best Rap Album in 2021?
A: Nas for "King's Disease"

Q: What film won the Best Picture Oscar in 2012?
A: The Artist

Q: Who won the Emmy for Outstanding Lead Actor in a Comedy Series in 2019?
A: Bill Hader for "Barry"

Q: Which actor made a memorable acceptance speech at the Oscars by dedicating it to "any kid who is being bullied"?
A: Graham Moore

Q: What film won the Best Picture Oscar in 1984?
A: Amadeus

Q: Who won the Grammy for Best New Artist in 2019?
A: Dua Lipa

Q: Which director won the Best Director Oscar for "The Departed"?
A: Martin Scorsese

Q: What movie won the Best Animated Feature Oscar in 2019?
A: Spider-Man: Into the Spider-Verse

Q: Who won the Emmy for Outstanding Lead Actress in a Comedy Series in 2020?
A: Catherine O'Hara for "Schitt's Creek"

Q: Which actress gave an emotional acceptance speech at the Oscars by saying, "This moment is so much bigger than me"?
A: Halle Berry

Q: What film won the Best Picture Oscar in 2007?
A: The Departed

Q: Who won the Grammy for Record of the Year in 2018?
A: Bruno Mars for "24K Magic"

Q: What actor has hosted the Oscars the most times?
A: Bob Hope

Q: Which film won the Best Picture Oscar in 2015?
A: Birdman

Q: Who won the Emmy for Outstanding Supporting Actor in a Drama Series in 2019?
A: Peter Dinklage for "Game of Thrones"

Q: Which artist gave a memorable acceptance speech at the Grammys by saying, "I'm going to let you finish, but..."?
A: Kanye West

Q: What film won the Best Picture Oscar in 1991?
A: The Silence of the Lambs

Q: Who won the Grammy for Best Pop Vocal Album in 2021?

A: Dua Lipa for "Future Nostalgia"

Q: Which film won the Best Picture Oscar in 1997?
A: The English Patient

Q: Who won the Emmy for Outstanding Lead Actor in a Drama Series in 2017?
A: Sterling K. Brown for "This Is Us"

Q: Which actor made headlines by jumping on Oprah Winfrey's couch during an interview?
A: Tom Cruise

Q: What film won the Best Picture Oscar in 2002?
A: A Beautiful Mind

Q: Who won the Grammy for Song of the Year in 2020?
A: Billie Eilish for "Bad Guy"

Q: Which director won the Best Director Oscar for "Schindler's List"?
A: Steven Spielberg

Q: What film won the Best Picture Oscar in 2010?
A: The Hurt Locker

Q: Who won the Emmy for Outstanding Lead Actress in a Limited Series in 2020?
A: Regina King for "Watchmen"

Q: Which actress made headlines at the Oscars by wearing a swan dress?
A: Björk

Q: What film won the Best Picture Oscar in 1989?

A: Rain Man

Q: Who won the Grammy for Album of the Year in 2018?
A: Bruno Mars for "24K Magic"

Q: Which actor gave a memorable acceptance speech at the Oscars by asking people to donate to a charity?
A: Matthew McConaughey

Q: What film won the Best Picture Oscar in 2006?
A: Crash

Q: Who won the Emmy for Outstanding Lead Actor in a Limited Series in 2019?
A: Jharrel Jerome for "When They See Us"

Q: Which actress made headlines at the Golden Globes by wearing a tuxedo instead of a dress?
A: Diane Keaton

Q: What film won the Best Picture Oscar in 2013?
A: Argo

Q: Who won the Grammy for Best Rock Album in 2021?
A: The Strokes for "The New Abnormal"

Q: Which director won the Best Director Oscar for "La La Land"?
A: Damien Chazelle

Q: What film won the Best Picture Oscar in 1981?
A: Chariots of Fire

Q: Who won the Emmy for Outstanding Lead Actress in a Drama Series in 2019?
A: Jodie Comer for "Killing Eve"

Q: Which actor made headlines by refusing their Oscar in 1973?
A: Marlon Brando

Q: What film won the Best Picture Oscar in 1993?
A: Unforgiven

Q: Who won the Grammy for Best Dance Recording in 2021?
A: Kaytranada featuring Kali Uchis for "10%"

Q: Which film won the Best Picture Oscar in 2005?
A: Million Dollar Baby

Q: Who won the Emmy for Outstanding Supporting Actress in a Comedy Series in 2020?
A: Annie Murphy for "Schitt's Creek"

Q: Which actor made headlines by thanking his horse in his Golden Globe acceptance speech?
A: Ricky Gervais

Q: What film won the Best Picture Oscar in 1995?
A: Braveheart

Q: Who won the Grammy for Record of the Year in 2017?
A: Adele for "Hello"

Q: Which director won the Best Director Oscar for "Life of Pi"?
A: Ang Lee

Q: What film won the Best Picture Oscar in 1985?
A: Out of Africa

Q: Who won the Emmy for Outstanding Lead Actor in a Comedy Series in 2020?
A: Eugene Levy for "Schitt's Creek"

Q: Which actress made headlines at the Emmys by wearing a bulletproof vest dress?
A: Jenifer Lewis

Q: What film won the Best Picture Oscar in 1982?
A: Gandhi

Q: Who won the Grammy for Best R&B Album in 2021?
A: John Legend for "Bigger Love"

Q: Which actor won an Oscar for their role in "The Revenant"?
A: Leonardo DiCaprio

Q: What film won the Best Picture Oscar in 1988?
A: The Last Emperor

Q: Who won the Emmy for Outstanding Lead Actress in a Limited Series in 2019?
A: Michelle Williams for "Fosse/Verdon"

Q: Which actor made headlines by declaring "I'm the king of the world!" during their Oscar acceptance speech?
A: James Cameron

Q: What film won the Best Picture Oscar in 1992?

A: The Silence of the Lambs

Q: Who won the Grammy for Best Country Album in 2021?
A: Miranda Lambert for "Wildcard"

Q: Which director won the Best Director Oscar for "Parasite"?
A: Bong Joon-ho

Q: What film won the Best Picture Oscar in 1986?
A: Platoon

Q: Who won the Emmy for Outstanding Lead Actor in a Limited Series in 2020?
A: Mark Ruffalo for "I Know This Much Is True"

Q: Which actress made headlines by kissing Halle Berry at the MTV Movie Awards?
A: Adrien Brody

Q: What film won the Best Picture Oscar in 1990?
A: Driving Miss Daisy

Q: Who won the Grammy for Best Pop Duo/Group Performance in 2021?
A: Lady Gaga and Ariana Grande for "Rain on Me"

Q: Which film won the Best Picture Oscar in 1996?
A: The English Patient

Q: Who won the Emmy for Outstanding Supporting Actor in a Comedy Series in 2020?
A: Daniel Levy for "Schitt's Creek"

Q: Which actor made headlines by mooning the
audience at the Golden Globes?
A: Jim Carrey

Food and Drink Pop Culture Trivia

Pop culture's fascination with celebrity chefs, fine dining, and popular cocktails reflects a growing appreciation for culinary arts and gastronomy.

Celebrity chefs like Gordon Ramsay and Anthony Bourdain have become household names, known for their culinary expertise and charismatic personalities showcased on TV shows and social media. Fine dining experiences and Michelin-starred restaurants captivate food enthusiasts, setting trends in cuisine and dining experiences. Popular cocktails, from classic martinis to trendy craft concoctions, evolve with mixology trends and social settings, becoming symbols of sophistication and cultural indulgence.

Together, these elements form a vibrant tapestry that celebrates culinary innovation and indulgence in contemporary pop culture.

Q: Which celebrity chef is known for shouting "Bam!" while cooking?
A: Emeril Lagasse

Q: What is the main ingredient in a traditional margarita?
A: Tequila

Q: Which country is the origin of the beer brand Guinness?
A: Ireland

Q: What type of wine is typically used in making sangria?
A: Red wine

Q: Who is the famous chef behind the restaurant "Hell's Kitchen"?
A: Gordon Ramsay

Q: What spirit is used in a classic mojito?
A: Rum

Q: Which chef is known for the phrase "Yes, chef!" and for his appearances on "MasterChef"?
A: Gordon Ramsay

Q: What is the main ingredient in a traditional Caesar salad dressing?
A: Anchovies

Q: What is the base spirit of a martini?
A: Gin or vodka

Q: Which beer is often referred to as "the king of beers"?
A: Budweiser

Q: Who is the chef behind the famous restaurant "Noma" in Copenhagen?
A: René Redzepi

Q: What cocktail is made with bourbon, sugar, and bitters?

A: Old Fashioned

Q: Which wine is known for its sparkling quality and is often associated with celebrations?
A: Champagne

Q: Who is the Italian-American chef famous for the phrase "That's a spicy meatball"?
A: Chef Boyardee (Hector Boiardi)

Q: What fruit is used to make traditional guacamole?
A: Avocado

Q: What is the main spirit in a cosmopolitan cocktail?
A: Vodka

Q: Which beer is known for its green bottle and red star logo?
A: Heineken

Q: Who is the British chef known for the TV show "The Naked Chef"?
A: Jamie Oliver

Q: What is the primary ingredient in hummus?
A: Chickpeas

Q: What spirit is used in a classic daiquiri?
A: Rum

Q: Which country is famous for its production of sake?
A: Japan

Q: Who is the chef behind the French Laundry restaurant in Napa Valley?
A: Thomas Keller

Q: What type of pasta is shaped like small rice grains and often used in soups?
A: Orzo

Q: What is the base spirit in a Bloody Mary?
A: Vodka

Q: Which beer is known as the world's oldest continuously operating brewery?
A: Weihenstephan

Q: Who is the host of the TV show "Diners, Drive-Ins and Dives"?
A: Guy Fieri

Q: What is the main ingredient in tzatziki sauce?
A: Yogurt

Q: What spirit is used in a traditional mint julep?
A: Bourbon

Q: Which country is the largest producer of wine in the world?
A: Italy

Q: Who is the celebrity chef known for the catchphrase "Kick it up a notch"?
A: Emeril Lagasse

Q: What is the key ingredient in a classic French bouillabaisse?
A: Fish

Q: What spirit is used in a traditional Negroni cocktail?
A: Gin

Q: Which beer is known for its association with the Australian Outback?
A: Foster's

Q: Who is the chef and television personality behind the show "30 Minute Meals"?
A: Rachael Ray

Q: What type of cheese is traditionally used in a Greek salad?
A: Feta

Q: What spirit is used in a traditional piña colada?
A: Rum

Q: Which country is famous for its production of Chianti wine?
A: Italy

Q: Who is the chef known for his molecular gastronomy techniques and the restaurant El Bulli?
A: Ferran Adrià

Q: What is the main ingredient in a traditional Italian risotto?
A: Arborio rice

Q: What spirit is used in a classic Moscow mule?
A: Vodka

Q: Which beer brand is known for its blue ribbon and American heritage?
A: Pabst Blue Ribbon

Q: Who is the chef and host of the TV show "Good Eats"?
A: Alton Brown

Q: What is the key ingredient in a traditional Middle Eastern tabbouleh?
A: Bulgur wheat

Q: What spirit is used in a classic Manhattan cocktail?
A: Whiskey

Q: Which country is known for producing Malbec wine?
A: Argentina

Q: Who is the celebrity chef known for his role on "Iron Chef America" and "Restaurant: Impossible"?
A: Robert Irvine

Q: What type of fish is traditionally used in fish and chips?
A: Cod

Q: What spirit is used in a classic tequila sunrise?
A: Tequila

Q: Which beer is known for its distinctive black can and harp logo?
A: Guinness

Q: Who is the chef behind the restaurant "Momofuku"?
A: David Chang

Q: What is the primary ingredient in a classic Italian bruschetta?
A: Tomatoes

Q: What spirit is used in a classic gin and tonic?
A: Gin

Q: Which country is famous for its production of
Rioja wine?
A: Spain

Q: Who is the chef and host of the TV show
"Barefoot Contessa"?
A: Ina Garten

Q: What type of bread is traditionally used to make a
Reuben sandwich?
A: Rye

Q: What spirit is used in a classic Mai Tai?
A: Rum

Q: Which beer is known for its association with
Mexican culture and Cinco de Mayo?
A: Corona

Q: Who is the chef known for his Southern cuisine
and the restaurant "The Lady & Sons"?
A: Paula Deen

Q: What is the main ingredient in a traditional Indian
biryani?
A: Rice

Q: What spirit is used in a classic screwdriver cocktail?
A: Vodka

Q: Which country is famous for its production of
Sauvignon Blanc wine?

A: New Zealand

Q: Who is the chef known for his work at the restaurant "The French Laundry"?
A: Thomas Keller

Q: What type of pasta is shaped like small, elongated shells and often used in macaroni and cheese?
A: Elbow macaroni

Q: What spirit is used in a classic whiskey sour?
A: Whiskey

Q: Which beer is known for its iconic red and white label and Canadian origin?
A: Molson Canadian

Q: Who is the chef and television personality known for his phrase "Good Eats"?
A: Alton Brown

Q: What is the main ingredient in a traditional Japanese miso soup?
A: Miso paste

Q: What spirit is used in a classic Tom Collins cocktail?
A: Gin

Q: Which country is famous for its production of Shiraz wine?
A: Australia

Q: Who is the chef behind the famous restaurant "Spago"?
A: Wolfgang Puck

Q: What type of cheese is traditionally used in a classic Italian lasagna?
A: Ricotta

Q: What spirit is used in a classic Paloma cocktail?
A: Tequila

Q: Which beer is known for its connection to the Netherlands and its green bottle?
A: Heineken

Q: Who is the chef and television personality known for her "30 Minute Meals"?
A: Rachael Ray

Q: What is the primary ingredient in a traditional Spanish paella?
A: Rice

Q: What spirit is used in a classic White Russian cocktail?
A: Vodka

Q: Which country is famous for its production of Prosecco?
A: Italy

Q: Who is the chef known for his show "Good Eats" and his scientific approach to cooking?
A: Alton Brown

Q: What is the main ingredient in a traditional Greek moussaka?
A: Eggplant

Q: What spirit is used in a classic Singapore Sling?

A: Gin

Q: Which beer is known for its connection to Belgian abbey traditions?
A: Chimay

Q: Who is the chef and owner of the restaurant "Alinea" in Chicago?
A: Grant Achatz

Q: What is the primary ingredient in a traditional German sauerkraut?
A: Cabbage

Q: What spirit is used in a classic Black Russian cocktail?
A: Vodka

Q: Which country is famous for its production of Port wine?
A: Portugal

Q: Who is the chef known for his show "Essence of Emeril"?
A: Emeril Lagasse

Q: What type of pasta is shaped like bow ties and often used in pasta salads?
A: Farfalle

Q: What spirit is used in a classic Sazerac cocktail?
A: Rye whiskey

Q: Which beer is known for its black and gold can and Jamaican origin?
A: Red Stripe

Q: Who is the chef and owner of the restaurant "Chez Panisse" in Berkeley?
A: Alice Waters

Q: What is the primary ingredient in a traditional Middle Eastern falafel?
A: Chickpeas

Q: What spirit is used in a classic Brandy Alexander cocktail?
A: Brandy

Q: Which country is famous for its production of Riesling wine?
A: Germany

Q: Who is the chef and television personality known for her show "Barefoot Contessa"?
A: Ina Garten

Q: What type of cheese is traditionally used in a French croque-monsieur?
A: Gruyère

Q: What spirit is used in a classic Daiquiri cocktail?
A: Rum

Q: Which beer is known for its connection to Mexican culture and its clear bottle?
A: Corona

Q: Who is the chef and restaurateur behind the "Momofuku" restaurant group?
A: David Chang

Q: What is the primary ingredient in a traditional Japanese tempura batter?
A: Flour

Q: What spirit is used in a classic Sidecar cocktail?
A: Brandy

Technology and Gadgets Pop Culture Trivia

Pop culture's fascination with technology revolves around our constant quest for innovation and convenience.

From smartphones to smart homes, gadgets shape our daily lives and cultural norms. Tech giants like Apple and Tesla drive trends, while social media and streaming platforms redefine how we connect, consume content, and define modern lifestyles.

Q: Who is the co-founder of Microsoft along with Bill Gates?
A: Paul Allen

Q: What was the first smartphone released by Apple called?
A: iPhone

Q: Which company developed the first commercial microprocessor?
A: Intel

Q: What is the name of the robot vacuum cleaner developed by iRobot?
A: Roomba

Q: Who invented the World Wide Web?

A: Tim Berners-Lee

Q: What does GPS stand for?
A: Global Positioning System

Q: Which company is known for its "Think Different" advertising campaign?
A: Apple

Q: What was the first gaming console released by Sony?
A: PlayStation

Q: Who is known as the father of the modern computer?
A: Alan Turing

Q: Which tech company was founded in a garage in Palo Alto by two college friends?
A: Hewlett-Packard (HP)

Q: What was the first successful personal computer sold by IBM?
A: IBM PC

Q: Who is the inventor of the first practical telephone?
A: Alexander Graham Bell

Q: What does LED stand for in lighting technology?
A: Light Emitting Diode

Q: Which company developed the first mass-produced electric car, the Model S?
A: Tesla

Q: Who co-founded Google with Sergey Brin?
A: Larry Page

Q: What year was the first version of Microsoft Windows released?
A: 1985

Q: What is the name of Amazon's virtual assistant?
A: Alexa

Q: Who is the CEO of SpaceX and Tesla?
A: Elon Musk

Q: What is the primary programming language used to develop Android apps?
A: Java

Q: What was the first handheld mobile phone model released by Motorola?
A: DynaTAC 8000X

Q: Which company is known for its search engine and has the motto "Don't be evil"?
A: Google

Q: Who is the founder of Facebook?
A: Mark Zuckerberg

Q: What year was the first iPad released?
A: 2010

Q: What does VPN stand for in network technology?
A: Virtual Private Network

Q: Which tech company is known for its Surface line of tablets and laptops?
A: Microsoft

Q: What is the name of the first computer virus ever created?
A: Creeper

Q: Who is credited with creating the first mechanical computer, the Analytical Engine?
A: Charles Babbage

Q: What is the primary function of a GPU in a computer?
A: Graphics Processing Unit (to render images and videos)

Q: Which company launched the first commercial website in 1991?
A: CERN

Q: What does SSD stand for in data storage technology?
A: Solid State Drive

Q: Who is the co-founder and former CEO of Apple known for his role in revolutionizing personal computing?
A: Steve Jobs

Q: What was the first successful home video game console released by Atari?
A: Atari 2600

Q: Which company developed the first commercially successful graphical user interface (GUI) computer, the Macintosh?
A: Apple

Q: What is the name of the virtual reality headset developed by Oculus VR?
A: Oculus Rift

Q: Who invented the first email system?
A: Ray Tomlinson

Q: What year was the first version of the Android operating system released?
A: 2008

Q: What does IoT stand for in technology?
A: Internet of Things

Q: Which tech company is known for its flagship Galaxy line of smartphones?
A: Samsung

Q: Who is the founder of Amazon?
A: Jeff Bezos

Q: What was the name of the first graphical web browser?
A: Mosaic

Q: What does RAM stand for in computer hardware?
A: Random Access Memory

Q: Which company is known for its innovative action cameras, such as the HERO series?
A: GoPro

Q: Who developed the first successful personal computer, the Apple I?
A: Steve Wozniak

Q: What year was the first commercially available CD player released?
A: 1982

Q: What does AI stand for in technology?
A: Artificial Intelligence

Q: Which company developed the popular video game series "Halo"?
A: Bungie

Q: Who is known as the "mother of computing" and developed the first compiler for a computer programming language?
A: Grace Hopper

Q: What is the name of the first portable music player developed by Apple?
A: iPod

Q: Which company developed the first commercially successful tablet computer, the iPad?
A: Apple

Q: What does HTTP stand for in web technology?
A: HyperText Transfer Protocol

Q: Who is the inventor of the first mechanical mouse?
A: Douglas Engelbart

Q: What year was the first public release of the Linux operating system?
A: 1991

Q: What is the name of Google's mobile operating system?

A: Android

Q: Which company developed the first digital camera?
A: Kodak

Q: Who is the co-founder of Twitter and its first CEO?
A: Jack Dorsey

Q: What does USB stand for in computer hardware?
A: Universal Serial Bus

Q: Which company is known for its innovative electric scooters and hoverboards?
A: Segway

Q: Who is the founder of Oracle Corporation?
A: Larry Ellison

Q: What year was the first successful transatlantic telegraph cable completed?
A: 1866

Q: What does VR stand for in gaming and technology?
A: Virtual Reality

Q: Which company developed the first successful smartwatch, the Apple Watch?
A: Apple

Q: Who is the inventor of the first practical incandescent light bulb?
A: Thomas Edison

Q: What year was the first public release of the Mozilla Firefox web browser?
A: 2004

Q: What does HTML stand for in web development?
A: HyperText Markup Language

Q: Which company developed the first commercially successful drone for consumers, the Phantom series?
A: DJI

Q: Who is the co-founder of WhatsApp?
A: Jan Koum

Q: What year was the first text message sent?
A: 1992

Q: What does RFID stand for in technology?
A: Radio Frequency Identification

Q: Which company is known for its flagship ThinkPad line of laptops?
A: Lenovo

Q: Who is the inventor of the first practical digital camera?
A: Steven Sasson

Q: What year was the first public release of the Google Chrome web browser?
A: 2008

Q: What does HTTP stand for in web technology?
A: HyperText Transfer Protocol

Q: Which company developed the first commercially successful 3D printer?
A: Stratasys

Q: Who is the founder of Alibaba Group?
A: Jack Ma

Q: What year was the first successful transatlantic telephone call made?
A: 1927

Q: What does OLED stand for in display technology?
A: Organic Light Emitting Diode

Q: Which company developed the first successful cloud storage service, Dropbox?
A: Dropbox Inc.

Q: Who is the co-founder of Tesla, Inc. along with Elon Musk?
A: Martin Eberhard

Q: What year was the first public release of the Windows operating system?
A: 1985

Q: What does SQL stand for in database management?
A: Structured Query Language

Q: Which company is known for its innovative electric vehicles, including the Leaf?
A: Nissan

Q: Who is the inventor of the first practical mechanical calculator, the Pascaline?
A: Blaise Pascal

Q: What year was the first public release of the Macintosh computer?
A: 1984

Q: What does GUI stand for in computing?
A: Graphical User Interface

Q: Which company developed the first successful e-reader, the Kindle?
A: Amazon

Q: Who is the co-founder of YouTube along with Steve Chen and Jawed Karim?
A: Chad Hurley

Q: What year was the first public release of the Android operating system?
A: 2008

Q: What does API stand for in software development?
A: Application Programming Interface

Q: Which company developed the first successful home video game console, the Atari 2600?
A: Atari

Q: Who is the founder of Microsoft?
A: Bill Gates

Q: What year was the first public release of the Linux operating system?
A: 1991

Q: What does URL stand for in web technology?
A: Uniform Resource Locator

Q: Which company developed the first successful action camera, the GoPro?
A: GoPro

Q: Who is the inventor of the first mechanical television?
A: John Logie Baird

Q: What year was the first public release of the Java programming language?
A: 1995

Q: What does CPU stand for in computing?
A: Central Processing Unit

Q: Which company developed the first commercially successful electric scooter, the Segway?
A: Segway Inc.

Q: Who is the co-founder of WhatsApp along with Jan Koum?
A: Brian Acton

Q: What year was the first public release of the Mozilla Firefox web browser?
A: 2004

Q: What does SSL stand for in web security?
A: Secure Sockets Layer

What Celebrities Love Pop Culture Trivia

Pop culture's obsession with celebrity gossip delves into stars' personal lives, from relationships to extravagant lifestyles.

Social media amplifies their daily routines and endorsements, shaping trends in fashion, beauty, and leisure activities. Paparazzi snapshots and tabloid headlines fuel a continuous cycle of fascination and scrutiny over their every move.

Q: Which celebrity is known for their love of beekeeping?
A: Morgan Freeman

Q: Which actor has a passion for painting and has released several art books?
A: Jim Carrey

Q: What sport does actress Kaley Cuoco actively participate in?
A: Horse riding

Q: Which musician is an avid fan of World of Warcraft?
A: Mila Kunis

Q: What is Oprah Winfrey's favorite book?
A: "To Kill a Mockingbird" by Harper Lee

Q: Which actor has a collection of typewriters?
A: Tom Hanks

Q: Which famous director enjoys making wine in his free time?
A: Francis Ford Coppola

Q: What hobby does actress Zooey Deschanel enjoy that involves crafting?
A: Knitting

Q: What is Emma Watson's favorite book?
A: "The Remains of the Day" by Kazuo Ishiguro

Q: Which actor is known for his love of motorcycles and even owns his own motorcycle company?
A: Keanu Reeves

Q: Which celebrity enjoys fencing as a recreational activity?
A: Will Smith

Q: What sport is singer Justin Timberlake known to be passionate about?
A: Golf

Q: What quirky hobby does actress Kristen Bell have?
A: Collecting sloths

Q: Which actor is a licensed pilot and owns several planes?
A: Harrison Ford

Q: What is Taylor Swift's favorite TV show?
A: "Friends"

Q: Which famous musician is also a skilled painter, often creating album art?
A: Joni Mitchell

Q: What unusual pet does actor Nicolas Cage own?
A: A two-headed snake

Q: Which actress loves playing board games, especially Settlers of Catan?
A: Kristen Bell

Q: What is actor Leonardo DiCaprio's favorite book?
A: "The Great Gatsby" by F. Scott Fitzgerald

Q: Which celebrity enjoys gardening and has written books on the subject?
A: Martha Stewart

Q: What is actress Reese Witherspoon's favorite movie?
A: "Gone with the Wind"

Q: Which actor is an avid snowboarder?
A: Samuel L. Jackson

Q: What hobby does singer Shakira enjoy that involves physical activity?
A: Belly dancing

Q: Which famous director has a passion for collecting movie memorabilia?
A: Steven Spielberg

Q: What is Jennifer Lawrence's favorite TV show?
A: "Keeping Up with the Kardashians"

Q: Which celebrity loves playing chess and participates in tournaments?
A: Madonna

Q: What sport does actor Matthew McConaughey enjoy playing?
A: Football

Q: Which actress has a passion for archery?
A: Geena Davis

Q: What is singer Beyoncé's favorite movie?
A: "A Star is Born"

Q: Which actor has a collection of vintage comic books?
A: Nicolas Cage

Q: What quirky habit does singer Lady Gaga have when preparing for a performance?
A: Burning sage

Q: Which celebrity is known for their love of yachting?
A: Leonardo DiCaprio

Q: What is singer Adele's favorite TV show?
A: "The X Factor"

Q: Which famous chef is an avid cyclist?
A: Gordon Ramsay

Q: What hobby does actor Johnny Depp enjoy that involves creativity?
A: Playing the guitar

Q: Which actress is known for her passion for baking?

A: Blake Lively

Q: What is actor Dwayne "The Rock" Johnson's favorite sport?
A: Football

Q: Which musician has a collection of guitars and often customizes them?
A: Eric Clapton

Q: What quirky habit does actress Cameron Diaz have regarding health?
A: Sunbathing to boost her immune system

Q: Which celebrity enjoys surfing in their free time?
A: Chris Hemsworth

Q: What is actor Tom Cruise's favorite movie?
A: "To Kill a Mockingbird"

Q: Which actress has a passion for interior design?
A: Ellen Pompeo

Q: What sport does singer Justin Bieber enjoy playing?
A: Ice hockey

Q: Which actor is known for his love of photography?
A: Jeff Bridges

Q: What quirky habit does actress Jennifer Aniston have regarding food?
A: Eating the same salad every day for lunch

Q: Which celebrity enjoys hiking and often shares photos of their adventures?
A: Julianne Hough

Q: What is singer Rihanna's favorite book?
A: "The Tao of Pooh" by Benjamin Hoff

Q: Which actor has a collection of classic cars?
A: Jay Leno

Q: What sport does actress Eva Longoria enjoy playing?
A: Tennis

Q: Which celebrity loves playing the piano in their free time?
A: Hugh Laurie

Q: What quirky habit does actor Ryan Gosling have regarding travel?
A: Collecting souvenirs from every city he visits

Q: Which actress is known for her love of yoga?
A: Jennifer Aniston

Q: What is actor Robert Downey Jr.'s favorite movie?
A: "Harold and Maude"

Q: Which musician enjoys fishing in their free time?
A: Brad Paisley

Q: What quirky hobby does actress Emma Stone have?
A: Collecting vinyl records

Q: Which celebrity loves playing basketball and has participated in celebrity games?
A: Justin Bieber

Q: What is singer Taylor Swift's favorite book?
A: "The Hunger Games" by Suzanne Collins

Q: Which actor enjoys woodworking as a hobby?
A: Nick Offerman

Q: What sport does actress Mila Kunis enjoy playing?
A: Golf

Q: Which celebrity has a passion for skiing?
A: Pierce Brosnan

Q: What quirky habit does singer Katy Perry have before a performance?
A: Brushing her teeth

Q: Which actress is known for her love of running marathons?
A: Natalie Dormer

Q: What is actor Chris Evans' favorite movie?
A: "The Goonies"

Q: Which celebrity enjoys scuba diving in their free time?
A: Sandra Bullock

Q: What sport does actor Zac Efron enjoy playing?
A: Rock climbing

Q: Which musician is known for their love of cooking and has released a cookbook?
A: Trisha Yearwood

Q: What quirky habit does actress Julia Roberts have regarding health?
A: Oil pulling

Q: Which celebrity enjoys horseback riding and owns several horses?
A: Kaley Cuoco

Q: What is singer Ed Sheeran's favorite TV show?
A: "The Simpsons"

Q: Which actor has a passion for playing video games?
A: Henry Cavill

Q: What sport does actress Jennifer Garner enjoy playing?
A: Soccer

Q: Which celebrity is known for their love of cycling and has participated in charity rides?
A: Patrick Dempsey

Q: What quirky hobby does actor Tom Hiddleston have?
A: Learning new languages

Q: Which actress enjoys swimming and often shares photos of her in the pool?
A: Jessica Alba

Q: What is actor Ryan Reynolds' favorite movie?
A: "Planes, Trains & Automobiles"

Q: Which celebrity enjoys playing poker and has participated in tournaments?
A: Ben Affleck

Q: What sport does singer Miley Cyrus enjoy playing?
A: Tennis

Q: Which musician has a collection of rare books?
A: Keith Richards

Q: What quirky habit does actress Kate Winslet have regarding travel?
A: Keeping a journal

Q: Which celebrity enjoys rock climbing and often shares photos of their climbs?
A: Jared Leto

Q: What is singer Ariana Grande's favorite book?
A: "Harry Potter" series by J.K. Rowling

Q: Which actor is known for their love of cooking and often shares recipes?
A: Stanley Tucci

Q: What sport does actress Kate Hudson enjoy playing?
A: Pilates

Q: Which celebrity enjoys playing golf and has participated in charity tournaments?
A: Alice Cooper

Q: What quirky hobby does actress Emma Watson have?
A: Learning new languages

Q: Which actor enjoys playing video games and has voiced characters in them?
A: Vin Diesel

Q: What sport does singer Shakira enjoy playing?
A: Tennis

Q: Which musician is known for their love of wine and owns a vineyard?
A: Sting

Q: What quirky habit does actress Angelina Jolie have regarding food?
A: Eating insects

Q: Which celebrity enjoys running and often shares photos of their runs?
A: Reese Witherspoon

Q: What is actor Matthew McConaughey's favorite book?
A: "The Greatest Salesman in the World" by Og Mandino

Q: Which musician enjoys playing chess and often participates in tournaments?
A: Bruce Springsteen

Q: What sport does actress Charlize Theron enjoy playing?
A: Golf

Q: Which celebrity enjoys painting and has held art exhibitions?
A: Lucy Liu

Q: What quirky habit does actor Robert Pattinson have regarding food?
A: Cooking using unusual methods

Q: Which actress enjoys doing puzzles in her free time?
A: Kristen Bell

Q: What is singer Billie Eilish's favorite TV show?
A: "The Office"

Q: Which actor enjoys playing basketball and has participated in charity games?
A: Will Smith

Q: What sport does actress Margot Robbie enjoy playing?
A: Ice hockey

Q: Which musician is known for their love of fishing and often shares photos of their catches?
A: Eric Clapton

Dream Vacation Pop Culture Trivia

Pop culture often highlights dream vacations at elite destinations like the Maldives, St. Barts, and Aspen.

These hotspots are frequented by the rich and famous, who seek luxurious resorts, exclusive beaches, and high-end amenities, shaping travel trends and inspiring wanderlust among fans and aspiring travelers worldwide.

Q: Which beach in Malibu is known for its celebrity homes and pristine sands?
A: Carbon Beach

Q: Which Caribbean island is a favorite vacation spot for celebrities like Beyoncé and Jay-Z?
A: Saint Barthelemy (St. Barts)

Q: What is the name of the famous casino resort in Monaco frequented by the elite?
A: Monte Carlo Casino

Q: Which luxurious ski resort in Colorado is popular among Hollywood stars?
A: Aspen

Q: Which island in the Maldives is known for its overwater villas and celebrity visitors?

A: Velaa Private Island

Q: What is the name of the upscale beach club in Mykonos known for its A-list clientele?
A: Nammos Beach Club

Q: Which famous Las Vegas casino resort is known for hosting top-tier entertainers and celebrities?
A: The Bellagio

Q: Which ski resort in Switzerland is renowned for its luxury and attracts many wealthy visitors?
A: St. Moritz

Q: What is the name of the high-end resort in Bora Bora known for its stunning views and luxurious accommodations?
A: Four Seasons Resort Bora Bora

Q: Which French Riviera beach town is known for its Film Festival and celebrity sightings?
A: Cannes

Q: What is the name of the exclusive resort in the Bahamas owned by the Atlantis Paradise Island?
A: The Cove Atlantis

Q: Which Italian island is famous for its beautiful coastline and celebrity visitors?
A: Capri

Q: What is the name of the luxury casino resort in Macau that is popular among the wealthy?
A: The Venetian Macao

Q: Which ski resort in Utah is known for its luxury amenities and celebrity visitors during the Sundance Film Festival?
A: Park City

Q: Which famous beach in Hawaii is known for its luxury hotels and celebrity guests?
A: Wailea Beach

Q: What is the name of the high-end resort in Fiji that is a favorite among celebrities?
A: Laucala Island Resort

Q: Which Mediterranean island is known for its glamorous nightlife and attracts many celebrities?
A: Ibiza

Q: What is the name of the iconic casino resort in Singapore that is known for its rooftop infinity pool?
A: Marina Bay Sands

Q: Which ski resort in British Columbia is known for its luxury chalets and celebrity visitors?
A: Whistler Blackcomb

Q: Which Caribbean island is known for its luxury resorts and has been visited by the Obamas?
A: Necker Island

Q: What is the name of the luxurious beach resort in the Turks and Caicos Islands known for its celebrity guests?
A: Amanyara

Q: Which beach in the Hamptons is known for its exclusivity and celebrity sightings?

A: East Hampton Main Beach

Q: What is the name of the upscale casino resort in Las Vegas known for its luxury shopping and celebrity chefs?
A: The Wynn Las Vegas

Q: Which Swiss ski resort is famous for its luxury hotels and annual film festival?
A: Gstaad

Q: What is the name of the exclusive resort in French Polynesia known for its overwater bungalows and celebrity guests?
A: The Brando

Q: Which luxury beach destination in Thailand is known for its pristine waters and high-end resorts?
A: Phuket

Q: What is the name of the luxury casino resort in Atlantic City known for its celebrity performances?
A: Borgata Hotel Casino & Spa

Q: Which ski resort in Austria is known for its luxury accommodations and attracts many wealthy visitors?
A: Kitzbühel

Q: Which Hawaiian island is known for its luxury resorts and has been a favorite vacation spot for Oprah Winfrey?
A: Maui

Q: What is the name of the exclusive resort in the Seychelles known for its luxurious villas and celebrity guests?

A: North Island

Q: Which famous beach in California is known for its celebrity homes and stunning views?
A: Malibu Beach

Q: What is the name of the luxury casino resort in Monaco that is a favorite among the rich and famous?
A: Hôtel de Paris Monte-Carlo

Q: Which ski resort in France is known for its luxury chalets and attracts many celebrities?
A: Courchevel

Q: What is the name of the high-end resort in Bora Bora known for its luxurious overwater bungalows?
A: St. Regis Bora Bora Resort

Q: Which beach destination in Mexico is known for its luxury resorts and celebrity visitors?
A: Cabo San Lucas

Q: What is the name of the upscale casino resort in Las Vegas known for its opulent design and celebrity guests?
A: The Venetian Las Vegas

Q: Which ski resort in Italy is famous for its luxury accommodations and attracts many wealthy visitors?
A: Cortina d'Ampezzo

Q: Which Caribbean island is known for its luxury resorts and has been visited by Prince Harry?
A: Barbados

Q: What is the name of the exclusive beach resort in the Maldives known for its overwater villas and celebrity guests?
A: Soneva Jani

Q: Which beach in the Hamptons is known for its exclusivity and has been frequented by Gwyneth Paltrow?
A: Sagaponack Beach

Q: What is the name of the luxury casino resort in Macau known for its extravagant design and celebrity performances?
A: Wynn Macau

Q: Which ski resort in Colorado is known for its luxury amenities and attracts many Hollywood stars?
A: Vail

Q: Which island in the Maldives is known for its luxurious resorts and has been a favorite vacation spot for the Beckhams?
A: One&Only Reethi Rah

Q: What is the name of the exclusive resort in the Bahamas known for its luxurious accommodations and celebrity guests?
A: The Ocean Club, A Four Seasons Resort

Q: Which famous beach in Miami is known for its luxury hotels and celebrity sightings?
A: South Beach

Q: What is the name of the high-end casino resort in Las Vegas known for its celebrity chef restaurants?
A: Caesars Palace

Q: Which ski resort in France is known for its luxury accommodations and attracts many wealthy visitors?
A: Val d'Isère

Q: Which Caribbean island is known for its luxury resorts and has been a favorite vacation spot for the Kardashians?
A: Turks and Caicos

Q: What is the name of the exclusive beach resort in the Seychelles known for its luxurious villas and celebrity guests?
A: Fregate Island Private

Q: Which beach in Malibu is known for its celebrity homes and stunning views?
A: Zuma Beach

Q: What is the name of the luxury casino resort in Monaco known for its opulence and celebrity guests?
A: Fairmont Monte Carlo

Q: Which ski resort in Switzerland is known for its luxury accommodations and attracts many wealthy visitors?
A: Verbier

Q: Which island in the Maldives is known for its luxurious resorts and has been a favorite vacation spot for Will Smith?
A: Cheval Blanc Randheli

Q: What is the name of the exclusive resort in the Bahamas known for its luxurious accommodations and celebrity guests?

A: Rosewood Baha Mar

Q: Which famous beach in California is known for its celebrity homes and beautiful views?
A: Laguna Beach

Q: What is the name of the luxury casino resort in Macau known for its extravagant design and celebrity performances?
A: Galaxy Macau

Q: Which ski resort in Colorado is known for its luxury amenities and attracts many Hollywood stars?
A: Beaver Creek

Q: Which island in the Maldives is known for its luxurious resorts and has been a favorite vacation spot for David Beckham?
A: Amilla Fushi

Q: What is the name of the exclusive beach resort in the Seychelles known for its luxurious villas and celebrity guests?
A: Six Senses Zil Pasyon

Q: Which beach in the Hamptons is known for its exclusivity and has been frequented by Alec Baldwin?
A: Main Beach, East Hampton

Q: What is the name of the luxury casino resort in Las Vegas known for its celebrity chef restaurants?
A: ARIA Resort & Casino

Q: Which ski resort in France is known for its luxury accommodations and attracts many wealthy visitors?
A: Megève

Q: Which Caribbean island is known for its luxury resorts and has been a favorite vacation spot for Justin Bieber?
A: Anguilla

Q: What is the name of the exclusive beach resort in the Maldives known for its luxurious overwater bungalows and celebrity guests?
A: Conrad Maldives Rangali Island

Q: Which beach in Malibu is known for its celebrity homes and stunning views?
A: Paradise Cove

Q: What is the name of the luxury casino resort in Monaco known for its opulence and celebrity guests?
A: Hôtel Hermitage Monte-Carlo

Q: Which ski resort in Switzerland is known for its luxury accommodations and attracts many wealthy visitors?
A: Zermatt

Q: Which island in the Maldives is known for its luxurious resorts and has been a favorite vacation spot for George Clooney?
A: Velaa Private Island

Q: What is the name of the exclusive resort in the Bahamas known for its luxurious accommodations and celebrity guests?
A: The Cove at Atlantis

Q: Which famous beach in California is known for its celebrity homes and beautiful views?

A: Santa Monica Beach

Q: What is the name of the luxury casino resort in
Macau known for its extravagant design and celebrity
performances?
A: City of Dreams

Q: Which ski resort in Colorado is known for its
luxury amenities and attracts many Hollywood stars?
A: Telluride

Q: Which island in the Maldives is known for its
luxurious resorts and has been a favorite vacation spot
for Leonardo DiCaprio?
A: Gili Lankanfushi

Q: What is the name of the exclusive beach resort in
the Seychelles known for its luxurious villas and
celebrity guests?
A: North Island

Q: Which beach in the Hamptons is known for its
exclusivity and has been frequented by Jerry Seinfeld?
A: Wainscott Beach

Q: What is the name of the luxury casino resort in Las
Vegas known for its celebrity chef restaurants?
A: The Cosmopolitan of Las Vegas

Q: Which ski resort in France is known for its luxury
accommodations and attracts many wealthy visitors?
A: Les Trois Vallées

Q: Which Caribbean island is known for its luxury
resorts and has been a favorite vacation spot for Drake?
A: Turks and Caicos

Q: What is the name of the exclusive beach resort in the Maldives known for its luxurious overwater bungalows and celebrity guests?
A: Soneva Fushi

Q: Which beach in Malibu is known for its celebrity homes and stunning views?
A: Broad Beach

Q: What is the name of the luxury casino resort in Monaco known for its opulence and celebrity guests?
A: Le Méridien Beach Plaza

Q: Which ski resort in Switzerland is known for its luxury accommodations and attracts many wealthy visitors?
A: Davos

Q: Which island in the Maldives is known for its luxurious resorts and has been a favorite vacation spot for Taylor Swift?
A: Anantara Kihavah Maldives Villas

Q: What is the name of the exclusive resort in the Bahamas known for its luxurious accommodations and celebrity guests?
A: The Ocean Club, A Four Seasons Resort

Q: Which famous beach in California is known for its celebrity homes and beautiful views?
A: Venice Beach

Q: What is the name of the luxury casino resort in Macau known for its extravagant design and celebrity performances?

A: Sands Macao

Q: Which ski resort in Colorado is known for its luxury amenities and attracts many Hollywood stars?
A: Snowmass

Q: Which island in the Maldives is known for its luxurious resorts and has been a favorite vacation spot for Selena Gomez?
A: COMO Cocoa Island

Q: What is the name of the exclusive beach resort in the Seychelles known for its luxurious villas and celebrity guests?
A: Denis Private Island

Q: Which beach in the Hamptons is known for its exclusivity and has been frequented by Steven Spielberg?
A: Georgica Beach

Q: What is the name of the luxury casino resort in Las Vegas known for its celebrity chef restaurants?
A: Mandalay Bay

Q: Which ski resort in France is known for its luxury accommodations and attracts many wealthy visitors?
A: Chamonix

Q: Which Caribbean island is known for its luxury resorts and has been a favorite vacation spot for Katy Perry?
A: Saint Lucia

Q: What is the name of the exclusive beach resort in the Maldives known for its luxurious overwater bungalows and celebrity guests?
A: Anantara Veli Maldives Resort

Q: Which beach in Malibu is known for its celebrity homes and stunning views?
A: Point Dume

Q: What is the name of the luxury casino resort in Monaco known for its opulence and celebrity guests?
A: Monte-Carlo Bay Hotel & Resort

Q: Which ski resort in Switzerland is known for its luxury accommodations and attracts many wealthy visitors?
A: Crans-Montana

Q: Which island in the Maldives is known for its luxurious resorts and has been a favorite vacation spot for Brad Pitt?
A: Baros Maldives

Q: What is the name of the exclusive resort in the Bahamas known for its luxurious accommodations and celebrity guests?
A: Grand Isle Resort & Spa

Q: Which famous beach in California is known for its celebrity homes and beautiful views?
A: Malibu Lagoon State Beach

9 798333 661074